Man-Trackers & Dog Handlers in Search & Rescue

Basic Guidelines and Information

D1604459

by

Gregory Fuller, Ed Johnson and Robert Koester

dbS

dbS Productions
Charlottesville, Virginia

Cover graphic: Gregory Fuller
Copy Editors: Laura D. Williams, Mary K. Hardy, Emily Powell Koester

Fig 3.1 Photo by Ron Jones
Fig 3.2- 3.4 courtesy of Ted Andrus
Fig 3.5, 4.1-4.3 Bob Koenig adapted from *Wilderness Search Strategy for Dog Handlers* courtesy of Marcia Koenig
Tracking Kit, Bibliography, and Tracker working with Canine Checklist (p82-89) courtesy of Greg Fuller & Leo Delaney
Quote by Charles Worsham (p. 19) from *Techniques of Tracking on Various Ground Covers* courtesy of Charles Worsham
Popsicle® is a registered Trademark of Good Humor-Breyers Ice Cream.

Published by dbS Productions LLC
P.O. Box 1894
Charlottesville, Virginia 22903
(800) 745-1891
www.dbs-sar.com

Printed in the United States

10 9 8 7 6 5 4 3 - Third Printing

Library of Congress Cataloging-in-Publication Data

Fuller, Gregory, 1946-
Man-trackers & dog handlers in search & rescue : basic guidelines and information / by
Gregory Fuller, Ed Johnson, Robert Koester.
    p. cm.
Includes bibliographical references and index.
ISBN 1-879471-30-2 (hbk. : alk. paper) -- ISBN 1-879471-31-0 (pbk : alk. paper)
1. Lifesaving. 2. Search and rescue operations. 3. Tracking and trailing. 4. Tracking
dogs. I. Title: Man-trackers and dog handlers in search and rescue. II. Johnson, Ed,
1948- III. Koester, Robert J. (Robert James), 1962- IV. Title

HV660+

00-025788

To Ranger, a search and rescue dog who gave his life
saving others.

Greg Fuller

To all of those who unselfishly shared their knowledge and
experience with me when I joined the SAR Community.

Ed Johnson

To search subjects who were not found in time,
their loved ones left behind,
all for lack of trained searchers and skilled management.

Robert J. Koester

The authors wish to express our sincere thanks to the listed contributors for reading many drafts, giving us their suggestions and additions, and helping us to reach out and promote the use of these two viable resources together. The combined experience, skill, and expertise of these specialists along with the suggestions, modifications, and additions provided by our expert reviewers have led to the creation of a comprehensive resource document that should be of great value to all search professionals.

Authors

Greg M. Fuller

Tracking Courses Developer, Technical Instructor - Virginia Department of Emergency Services
Director - Search and Rescue Tracking Institute
Tracker - Appalachian Search & Rescue Conference
Associate - Virginia Bloodhound Search and Rescue Association

Onancock, VA

Ed Johnson

Operational Dog Handler, Incident Commander - DOGS East (Ret.)
Technical Instructor - Virginia Department of Emergency Services
Associate - Search and Rescue Tracking Institute

King George, VA

Robert J. Koester

Incident Commander-Appalachian Search and Rescue Conference
President - Virginia Search and Rescue Council
Disaster Assistance Employee, Training Team Leader - FEMA
Incident Commander-Ground Developer, Technical Instructor, Disaster Reservist
Virginia Department of Emergency Services

Charlottesville, VA

Contributors and Reviewers

Mike Anderson
Search and Rescue Dog Association of Alberta
Alberta, Canada

Jennifer Applegate
Downeast Search and Rescue Dogs
Bar Harbor, Maine

Meg Birney
DOGS East
Falls Church, Virginia

Dan Comden
German Shepherd Search Dogs of Washington State
Lake Forest Park, Washington

Terry Davis
Virginia Bloodhound Search and Rescue Association
National Police Bloodhound Association
Leesburg, Virginia

Leo Delaney
Travis County SAR
Lost and Hound Foundation
Austin, Texas

J.R. Frost
Soza & Company, Ltd.
Fairfax, VA

Gabriele Hilgert
K-9 Alert
Chesterfield, Virginia

Derek Koonce
California Rescue Dog Assoc. 169
San Jose, California

Lisa Lee
California Rescue Dog Association,
LaHonda, California

Dwight McAtee
K-9 Alert
Richmond, Virginia

Steve McConaughy
Rescue Dogs, Inc.
Medford, Massachusetts

Kakie Moore
Florida Search and Rescue K-9
Tracking & Cadaver Recovery,
Palm Harbor, Florida

James P. O'Brien
NASAR
Las Vegas, Nevada

Edward Parham
Officer, Chesterfield Police
Chesterfield, Virginia

Billy L. Smith Sr.
CEO, Law Enforcement Training Specialist
Rosharon, Texas

Louis C. Villa
Sonoran Search and Rescue
Maricopa, Arizona

Kimberly Watson
Jack County Sheriff's Department
Jacksboro, Texas

Table of Contents

Appedixes

Preface

This material started as a very brief lecture for the course, *Field Team Signcutter* (FTS). The FTS course is a 50-hour introduction to the basic art, science, and skills of awareness, signcutting, and tracking. The Commonwealth of Virginia currently has certified over 100 FTS, resulting in more FTS searchers responding to searches. The ultimate goal is to get all searchers trained in signcutting and tracking. But, as with the growth of any program, new problems have surfaced.

Confusion and problems developed at a recent search, where ten FTS responded, and seven of them were placed with canine teams. In an attempt to be creative and get them into the field, management coupled them with canine handlers. It seemed like a good idea at the time. Neither the FTS nor the canine teams knew how to operate together efficiently or effectively. When analyzing these problems later, we realized that even though we discuss signcutting and tracking with canine teams in the FTS class, we had not been giving those beginning tracking students any in-depth information. The students need to know how a canine team might operate and what the canine team may expect from the tracking person. Likewise, canine handlers have not been educated about the training, tactics, or abilities of assigned trackers.

Because of the problems that had surfaced, we realized several important steps needed to be taken. The first was the proper cross education for both handlers and trackers. A major purpose of this book is to allow both specialists to begin to understand the tactics, skills, and limitations of each type of resource. The second step involves actual field training conducted together. The third is rational combined deployment on real searches.

This book began as a simple set of guidelines for trackers who might work with canines. However, it soon became apparent that in order for true teamwork to occur the information also had to be directed at canine handlers. The final step in the evolution of the book was the realization that it is ultimately a management decision to combine resources.

Over the years, the authors, an incident commander, a dog handler, and a tracker learned to put aside their differences and work together. Teamwork not only benefitted each resource, it clearly helped the lost subject. We are now steadfast in our belief that under the proper circumstances other regions of the country would also benefit from this combined tactic. If we have managed to not only get along, but also become great friends, then in can be repeated elsewhere.

For any book to improve, it must benefit from its users' suggestions. Since we all want the understanding and working relationship between these disciplines to improve and assist us in the field, it is requested that you contact the authors with any suggestions, comments, or additions for future revisions.

Greg Fuller
Tracking questions/comments
info@dbs-sar.com

Ed Johnson
Canine questions/comments
E760@aol.com

Robert J Koester
Management questions and editorial comments
robert@dbs-sar.com

1. Introduction

This book advocates and assists in combining trackers and handlers in the field. This book will also be useful for search managers in recognizing the value of combing these important **resources** under some circumstances. Past experience has clearly demonstrated the effectiveness of combining resources.

Missing Without Reason

It is a cold winter afternoon in the rolling hills of rural Virginia. A.G., a 70 year-old male on medication for depression, cannot be found. Family and friends are contacted to mount an impromptu search effort. Later, an emergency call rings in the county's 911 center requesting law enforcement assistance. A tracker and an air-scent dog are quickly assigned to search around the point last seen. Just as they deploy into the field, the radio breaks squelch. The team must move to a new site where family members located a bottle of prescription medication. Investigations just determined it belongs to A.G. Upon arriving at the new last known position, the search team sees several family members wandering around the clue. Nevertheless, the tracker locates one set of tracks that cannot be matched to the family members' shoe patterns. The track is sketched, photographed, measured, and sent back to base.

The tracker closely examines the tracks and determines a direction of travel heading north into the woods. The team's assignment changes to the new area. The air-scent dog takes the lead due to its ability to search a large area quickly. After 30 minutes of an open grid pattern the radio once again crackles into action. A hasty team a half-mile further north reports similar tracks. Base once again diverts the tracker and dog team to this new clue. The tracker quickly determines the measurements, shoe print pattern, and age of the tracks match.

The tracker takes the lead and finds both the direction of travel and the trail. The team employs the leap-frogging tactic to follow the trail for several hundred yards. As they enter into a new area with several dumpsters and a shed, the dog alerts. Teamwork and coordination allowed A.G. to be successfully located still alive in the shed.

This success only came about due to the previous training these two resources practiced long before this search. Over the years, a set of guidelines gradually developed. This book is generic and does not in any way try to describe or define a **signcutter**, signcutting, a **tracker**, tracking, **air-scent dog**, **dog handler**, or **scent-discriminating**. From the authors' research, it appears very evident that different regions have unique definitions, classifications, and terms, and these should be incorporated into a unit's working guidelines as necessary. Terms defined in the glossary appear in bold the first time they are used. These guidelines should be modified to the experience and skill level of the tracking person and canine team members. The authors decided to use the term *tracker* in this book to refer to the individual or team that finds or follows track or **sign** in the field. A highly scientific social experiment was conducted to make this determination: We asked a non-randomly selected eight-year-old what she called someone who finds or follows tracks. Her reply "a tracker" was rewarded with a cookie. Therefore, the term tracker is used throughout the text because it is the most generic term to describe someone willing to lay down in the mud at night and shine a flashlight at strange angles to see a tiny crease in a leaf. The term does not refer to the skill set or experience of this individual.

This book makes no attempt to decide the team leader: the dog handler, the tracking person, or another member of the team. This should be left up to either the team, the type of task assigned, local protocol, and/or base operations. There are many areas that utilize these disciplines differently. There are also many different schools of thought about the use of these resources. What is important is that both of these disciplines learn to operate together to assist each other in finding the lost or missing person. Common sense and teamwork must prevail.

It is highly recommended that any specialized resource, train with several different trackers or canine teams (air-scent and tracking/trailing) before operating in a real world situation where someone's life may be at stake. Also, it is recommended that canine team members train with tracking personnel whenever possible. This is not only the best way but the only way to prepare for the field. All searchers make mistakes in the field and should learn from them, but try to keep those mistakes minimal and preferably make them during training.

This book does not cover the tactics utilized for signcutting and tracking a criminal suspect. These are different from the tactics normally known and used by **search and rescue** (SAR) personnel. Trackers should stay away from this type of task unless they are law enforcement or military personnel. It is also critical that trackers have been taught by and trained with experienced tracking teachers on the different signcutting and tracking tactics required and on the inherent dangers of tracking criminal suspects.

> # WARNING:
> If you are a SAR volunteer, it is highly recommended that you abort your task when it is reported and/or verified that you are searching for a criminal suspect. **Tracking personnel have been killed!**

Assume that every **Point Last Seen** (PLS) or **Last Known Position** (LKP) is a possible crime scene and should be treated as such. Also, assume every search has the potential of turning into a criminal action. Indeed, any lost fearful subject may commit irrational if not dangerous actions towards a searcher. This is one of the inherent dangers of SAR. Avoid this danger by refusing to accept a task that is not recommended or when lacking proper training. Do not allow the "thrill of the chase" to override common sense and level of expertise!

This book attempts to address, on a limited platform, one of the many subjects in tracking that may have been overlooked. Hopefully this book will complement other tracking books, research, experience, and schooling. At the very least it should provoke thought and discussion.

The next chapter lays down the theoretical and statistical foundation of why management might choose to combine canine and tracking resources. Since the decision is often left up to search management, the chapter is largely written from their perspective. In order for field resources to work well together and gain trust they must understand the basic tactics each other use. Chapter Three discusses tracking awareness and tactics while Chapter Four explains canine resources and tactics. Next, Chapter Five brings together both resources by presenting information on how they can best communicate and work before, during, and after a field task. Unfortunately, a lot of resource information may have been learned through the movies. In order to dispel common myths and misconceptions, Chapter Six addresses tracking misunderstanding, while Chapter Seven tackles canine fallacies. The next two chapters present the skill sets that both of these search specialists should possess. While Chapters Ten and Eleven confront unfounded fears and concerns each resource may harbor. Finally, Chapter Twelve presents several exercises trackers and canine handlers may utilize for joint training.

Ultimately, the reader and user of this text determines if the information is of any benefit. The only way any book of this nature can be found beneficial and applicable is through time, use, and field testing.

2. Search Management's Perspective

Management deploys resources for the simple purpose of locating the lost subject in the shortest time. They also like to get all the field resources out into the field so they can drink all the coffee and eat all the food back at base. Operations research tells us to structure the deployment of available resources to maximize the overall probability of success (POS) in the shortest time.[1,2,3] This closely parallels an operational philosophy of safely finding the subject in the shortest time frame, with the most efficient type and number of resources, all while following applicable policies.[4] In other words, when the search manager/**incident commander** looks out into the staging area he tries to place the waiting resources into search areas that maximize the chance of a find with each passing minute.

Operations Research

Producing a search plan that attains the maximum chances of success in the minimum amount of time is a daunting task that requires search managers to juggle resource assignments with many other variables, most of which they cannot control. Some of these variables include **probability of area** (POA), **probability density** (Pden), **sweep width** (W), and search speed (V).[3,5,6,7] In reality, without a computer program the subject might turn to a skeleton before all the required calculations are completed and resources sent into the field.

The incident commander must be concerned with the big picture when supervising resource assignments. Assigning tasks to maximize overall success in the minimum amount of time is not always intuitively obvious. A tracker's task may place it in a segment where it will be less effective than if it were tasked to a second segment that best matched the tracker's capabilities in order to avoid assigning an air-scent dog to the second segment, when the dog team cannot search well in the second segment due to contamination. Such assignments, while not ideal for either resource when taken alone, could be the best way to find the subject in the shortest time. Under other circumstances, the best way to use two dissimilar resources might be to assign both of them to the same segment at the same time. This book concerns the latter situation when the two resources are trackers and handlers with their dogs.

Combining Resources

Putting formal search theory aside for a moment, the real reason to combine trackers and dogs is simply to find the subject faster. This combination represents for many a new concept and thus needs to be questioned. Using anecdotes to support the practice may appeal to many but does not satisfy a more rigid approach to modern SAR management.   No well-controlled research studies have clearly proved dog handlers and trackers must always work together. Indeed, under many circumstances these resources should not be combined.

Search theory is only able to support two theoretical justifications for combining trackers and handlers. The first situation involves a prediction that the probable success rate for the search is maximized by assigning these two resources to the same segment. This typically would require a search segment that has a high probability density, can be searched well by both resources (a highly simplified way of saying obtain a reasonable level of coverage), and/or one where the time factor may be more important than elsewhere (e.g., if the subject is in that particular segment, there is a greater chance that he is injured). The second justification involves when the incident commander has more resources than really needed to perform the specialized function (ten trackers show up at staging). In this case, mixing dissimilar resources in the same segment may increase effectiveness.

Some additional advantages of combining resources exist that cannot be easily calculated by the computers or SAR theorists.   Under some circumstances two dissimilar resources may provide nearly simultaneous verification of clues from two different perspectives. This often results in a newer, more accurate determination of POA which then immediately leads to a better deployment of resources and quicker finds. Another advantage is fewer tasks, less people, and quicker times for putting both resources into an area. However, all of these advantages must be carefully balanced against certain disadvantages.

It is critical for search planners to understand fixed rules do not exist for deciding when to combine resources. While formal search theory may suggest circumstances of resource combining, meaningful input of all the variables may be difficult at best. Subjective experience from hundreds of searches suggests the following guidelines. The best tracker or tracking team should be kept independent for initial work at the PLS, following up on tracks/sign reported by other teams, and utilizing the specialized tracking tactics described in Chapter Three. Only if additional tracking resources are available should they be tasked with tracking/trailing dogs. The independent verification of a track by the tracker and dog will almost always lead to a more refined POA. However, this type of tracking requires considerable skill and the special practice described in Chapter Twelve. Assigning trackers to air-scent dog teams is dependent upon many factors. Factors that suggest combining these resources include a large number of tracker resources, few discrete tracking tasks, deployment into a high POA segment, presence of track traps, or resources that have practiced together. Management is always free to consider other factors.

When air-scent dogs and trackers are combined, the dog team will usually serve as the primary resource. The purpose of combining the resources is to detect a wider range of clues in a shorter amount of time. Trackers are trained more in visual search than the typical searcher. Air-scent dogs make a significant number of finds. In Virginia 10-20% of finds for ground searches are attributed to air-scent dog teams.[8] However, a hidden truth is that often the walker/handler spots the subject. Clearly, a tracker who actively practices visual search techniques can further enhance the team. Air-scent dog teams are often assigned to areas based on their higher PODs under certain conditions. If indeed the subject has entered the search sector, sign should be present. If the tracker is able to spot this sign, even though the subject might be gone (therefore, no longer leaving scent for the dog to detect), the direction of the entire search may change.

In land searches, as opposed to maritime searches, the lost subject usually displays unique behavioral patterns. This means the PLS is usually precisely known and does not display the circular normal uncertainty common to reported positions in the middle of a featureless ocean.[2] Also unlike subjects adrift at sea, movement away from the PLS is not subject to winds and currents. Instead, the topography often gently pushes the lost subject into distinctive areas. Experienced search mangers, dog handlers, and trackers have learned the best places to look even within a single search sector. In some areas, the geography will form a *gate* that the subject must pass through. This allows the tracker to concentrate on a few key areas and not interfere with the air-scent task.

In many areas, the larger number of "trackers" with 24-50 hours of tracking awareness training results in trackers being paired with dog teams on a single task. This level of "tracker" makes an excellent walker with team member skills and visual search skills. However, at this level the "trackers" may lack the experience and comfort to rapidly track or cut for sign. Therefore, the trackers may easily become frustrated if they think their primary task is to signcut/track. Prior training or at least a clear explanation of the task from base is essential in this case.

Probability of Detection

The search manager may believe that a higher POD will be achieved by combining resources. Currently this somewhat reasonable hypothesis cannot be supported by any research. It has not been disproved, but simply no good ground POD research exists. Unlike the maritime or air search disciplines, the ground incident commander does not have the benefit of well-researched POD tables. Although two attempts using field experiments have been made to directly relate POD to searcher spacing for ground parties engaged in grid searches,[9,10] scientific research has shown that this is not an appropriate way to approach the problem of POD estimation.[1] In addition, the tactic of sweeping and grid searching should not be used until the later portions of more modern searches. Among trackers, hasty teams, **tracking dogs**, air-scent dogs, and **trailing dogs** only air-scent dogs have a putative POD table.[11] A closer examination of the table reveals it was not based upon actual field testing but instead relied upon personal gut instinct related to wind characteristics.

This lack of research poses a challenge to anyone trying to estimate PODs. Given current practices, team leaders know that upon returning from the field and sitting down across from a debriefing officer, they will face the ever present dilemma of estimating the POD for each specific task. Dog handlers face the extra burden of cross-species communication and analysis of the scent-carrying capacity of the wind. Unlike ground teams, the dog cannot easily admit it felt dehydrated halfway through the task and just could not get that juicy squirrel out of its mind. In the maritime search environment pilots now simply report the variables they can observe (e.g., wind speed and direction, sea state, visibility, true air-speed, time spent on scene searching, etc.). This allows the search planner to estimate the effective sweep widths for each of the possible search objects by using a table of "uncorrected" sweep widths and adjusting them with tabulated correction factors. Early during the maritime research project the researchers noticed the more specialized the resource the greater they overestimated their POD.[12] Few SAR resources have the opportunity to be part of a well-controlled SAR experiment that provides some meaningful feedback. Since these types of tables and graphs backed up by solid research do not exist for ground resources, no scientifically objective method exists for estimating POD for these resources. Therefore, current ground search planners must currently rely upon reported POD values that represent a team's best guess.

To understand the term *reported POD* better, a brief discussion of the POD concept is required. The POD for any given task is highly dependent upon the search object, the sensor (eyes, nose, ears, touch, radar, infrared, operator fatigue, etc.), environmental conditions in the segment, amount of effort spent in the area, and whether the searching effort was more-or-less uniformly distributed over the segment's area. Teams sometimes try to report a POD for the subject or for finding a smaller clue. However, in order for the POD x POA = POS equation to work properly the same target must be used for both the POA and POD.[1] In most lost person searches the search object is the subject. The prudent search manager will also apply a worst case scenario and make the POD calculations based on an unresponsive subject. This allows for a more reasonable overall POS$_{cumulative}$ objective, such as, conduct the search until a overall POS$_{cum}$ of X% is obtained. If the overall POS was based upon a responsive subject, the search might be suspended too early. The lost subject must have the benefit of the doubt.

The term POD often confuses field personnel and new staff members. A large part of this confusion is due to POD having several different contexts and the lack of objective methods for estimating its value in ground SAR. A POD can be predictive, reported, adjusted, theoretical, cumulative, or actual. Quite often a planning section chief or operations officer wants a chunk of area (we could argue over **segment** vs. **sector**) searched to a target POD.

Only two models have been published that would allow a grid/ sweep team to predict a specified POD.[9,13] In one model the author simply averaged results from day and night time tasks.[9] Any team leader knows the vast difference in search effectiveness for an object during the day and night. A planner, with no other more accurate tables, estimates required spacing to figure the number of resources required to complete the task within a specified amount of time. The field team leader could also use data from tables for that type of terrain or critical separation at the beginning of the task to meet management's POD objective for that task. Either system (critical separation or separation table) illustrates a **predictive POD**. LaValla and Stoffel also call this a **prospective POD** in their textbook.[14] Unfortunately, in both the dog and tracking worlds valid models that would allow an objective predictive POD estimate do not exist. Even if they did exist, the wide range of expertise and experiences that exists between different trackers and **dog teams** might be the most important variable.

Eventually, the team returns and gives the debriefing officer a reported POD. Hopefully this number is a meaningful estimate. An experienced team will report fatigue, terrain, wind characteristics, morale of the team, vegetation, search time, and many other factors. However, a trailing dog or tracker may report other factors more appropriate to detecting a scent trail or sign. Asking about the search conditions is important for the debriefing officer. While a reported estimate of POD may aid communication between the team leader and debriefer, it should not become part of a cumulative POD or POS calculation.

After the team debriefs, an experienced debriefing officer often looks at the reported POD estimate and adjusts it up or down subjectively based on the reported search conditions. This is especially common when receiving reports from inexperienced team leaders. Debriefers have received reports of a 95% POD for a two-hour task searching 160 acres of heavy brush from a three-person team when all other teams reported 5% PODs. The debriefer attempts to make the **adjusted POD** as reasonable as possible by adjusting it, usually downward, to better match the reported search conditions. The elusive goal is to make the adjusted POD better represent the actual POD. Some incident commanders have developed forms to calculate POD from information gathered from field personnel such as search speed, time spent searching, and sweep width estimates.[15] The adjusted POD is then used to calculate a **cumulative POD** (POD_{cum}).

Cumulative Probability of Detection

$$POD_{cum} = 1 - (1-POD_1)(1-POD_2)(1-POD_n)$$

The **actual POD** represents what the team would have actually found if there were in fact 100 subjects in the search area. This number can never be obtained. It requires repeated experiments under carefully controlled and monitored conditions. On actual searches most team members find nothing and will often begin to doubt the sanity of search management.

Resource Mixing

Understanding management's desire to use different types of resources in an area depends on an understanding of the difference between the results of formulas and the **actual POD$_{cum}$**. In calculating the POD$_{cum}$ search managers use the equation provided in the box above. The equation is based on probability theory, which tells us that the chances of two independent events both happening are the product of their probabilities. The important assumption in the equation is that both events are independent. In reality, most search planners do not use the formula but instead use a POD$_{cum}$ table found in search management reference books.[13] Remembering that this number represents a **theoretical POD$_{cum}$** is critical since it assumes the searching is independent. Comparable resources tend to search in a similar fashion and are not as independent as different resources. The practice of using different resources in a search area is sometimes referred to as **resource mixing**.

The more specialized the resource, the more unique its approach to searching. However, with benefits also come limitations. A helicopter cannot (or at least should not) fly underneath the forest canopy. A tracker simply cannot detect a subject a quarter-mile away if obscured by brush. An air-scent dog is going to be severely limited on a 105° F sunny day with no horizontal wind movement. Unfortunately, management seldom knows what the perfect resource is to detect that all-important clue.

> Combining dissimilar resources raises the chance of detecting different types of clues and simultaneous independent clue verification.
>
> This may lead to finding the subject faster if the teams are looking in the right place.

The more specialized the resource, the more resistant to working with some dissimilar resources. Often such complaints are valid. Having an air-scent dog stick its head out of a helicopter, while perhaps enjoyable for the dog, serves no real benefit. Anytime management attempts to combine resources it must be clear on both the objectives of the task and the reason for combining. Both tracking dogs and trackers are usually given the task of starting from the **initial planning point (IPP)**, attempting to detect an initial track/sign, and then following the track. However, the tracking dog will move at a rapid rate of speed, while the trackers may be much slower in their tactics. This represents a potential conflict. However, a skilled tracker added to the tracking dog's task can be a true asset. The experienced tracker can probably spot a confirmable track while moving at a high rate of speed that the dog handler may have missed. The tracker may also be able to put more emphasis on sign if they know it was not created by the dog or the handler. This type of information is invaluable to the management staff.

Clue Relevance

Two major factors determine the relevance of a clue in investigations: the source of the information and how well it falls into patterns supported by other clues. The value of a tracking dog trail depends on the **scent article**, PLS preservation, the dog's training, and tracking conditions. The experienced search manager has learned that not all tracks are valid. A single footprint, no matter how well it matches the subject's, must also be suspect. However, the combination of a hot track with the subject's footprint almost makes all of the math irrelevant. Indeed, this type of clue confirmation from dissimilar resources will most likely result in new POA calculations. Quite often, a trailing dog may get into a scent-pool area and have trouble working it out. This situation gives the man-tracker the opportunity to attempt to find sign and possibly follow it to the subject or help redirect the dog handler. In the above example, the tracking dog handler works its resource in the usual manner. The man-tracker is asked to be more flexible and attempt to track/signcut while moving quickly. This will often be the case since humans are theoretically more adaptable than animals.

Combining resources still represents a trade-off. The tracking resource does not function optimally unless they operate at their preferred speed, which generally is much slower than a dog team. In many circumstances it may make more sense to send the dog first and then the tracker. The disadvantage of this approach is time. The tracker cannot generally enter the air-scent dog handler's sector until the dog team is done. An air-scent dog team cannot enter an area a tracker is working until the tracker is done. The limitations of daylight and resources may require the follow up task to be delayed by a night or by a shift. A combined task only requires the dog, handler, and a tracker. Separate tasks would require an additional walker be placed with each team. However, management must be careful to explain the purpose of the task and priorities to both of the search specialists. Team members must have this information to ensure success. Combining resources represents a concurrent approach and, if done properly, should enhance the chances of finding the subject faster and hopefully still alive.

1. Koopman, B. (1980) *Search and Screening: General Principles with Historical Applications.* Pergamon Press, NY, NY.

2. Frost, J. (1998) *The Theory of Search: A Simplified Explanation.* Soza & Company & Office of Search and Rescue U.S. Coast Guard, Fairfax, VA.

3. Frost, J. (1999a) Principles of Search Theory, Part I: Detection. *Response.* 17:2:1-7.

4. Koester, R. (1996) *Field Operations Guide for Search & Rescue.* dbS Productions, Charlottesville, VA.

5. Frost, J. (1999b) Principles of Search Theory, Part II: Effort, Coverage, and POD. *Response.* 17:2:8-15.

6. Frost, J. (1999c) Principles of Search Theory, Part III: Probability Density Distributions. *Response.* 17:3:1-10.

7. Frost, J. (1999d) Principles of Search Theory, Part IV: Optimal effort Allocation. *Response.* 17:3:11-23.

8. Koester, R. (1998) The Lost Alzheimer's and Related Disorders Search Subject: New Research Perspectives. *NASAR Conference Proceedings.* NASAR Chantilly, VA.

9. Wartes, J. (1974) "An Experimental Analysis of Grid Sweep Searching" Washington State SAR

3. Tracking Resources & Tactics

This chapter seeks to give the non-tracking reader, dog handler, and experienced tracking person a new perspective and insight. Tracking is quite different from other SAR skills and disciplines. It requires developing and exercising a high level of visual intelligence, among other skills. Visual intelligence is quite similar to developing motor skills in that constant practice is required. It is impossible to teach how to track through the written media (this book). This is especially true since the purpose of this chapter is not to teach a tracker how to track. Instead, the goal is to allow the dog handler and management an overview of what the tracker faces to find those scratches in the dirt or creases on a leaf. However, very basic tracking guidelines will be discussed to help other personnel be more aware during tasks.

> Searchers must not lock-in to any one idea, tactic, or school of thought. Baselines and tactics should be continually changing. To "lock-in" or only follow "the book way to do it" could, at the least, cause people to not perform to their abilities.

The second half of the chapter presents several different tracking tactics. Many cannot be easily performed when working with a canine team. However, it is important for the canine handler to appreciate the different tactics the experienced tracker uses.

Baselines

The process of visual recognition relies on finding a small disturbance to the environment. Brighter light shining back from compressed ground or vegetation, a pebble kicked loose, these are the tracker's goals. But, to know what is different in the environment, the tracker must know every subtle nuance on intimate terms (environmental baseline). This requires both time and training to study the current environment.

The tracker must carefully determine the characteristics of the soil. Then he examines the ground cover. What was this environment like in the days before a potential foot impacted on this piece of ground? Temperature, moisture, and wind are all critical influences the skilled tracker considers. The lost subject's foot pounds upon the ground. Now the tracker must factor in all of the variables that were present before, during, and after the person was reported missing. Did the ground freeze during the intervening time? How did a cold wind dry the track out? The facts are revealed by careful study backed up by training. Environmental baselines change with each different soil, ground cover, time, and environmental factor. Therefore, the skilled tracker not only looks for sign but stops and reassess the environment on an almost continuous basis.

Baselines involve more than simply reading the current environment. Visual recognition involves putting vision on the target and then allowing the brain to analyze, process, and recognize the disturbance. For example, the tracker must look at a particular pine needle, and then through analysis and processing realize that it needs to be picked up, turned over, and examined for bruising. The tracker's brain must transform its visual recognition from the clutter of an urban/suburban environment to the subtle nuances of nature. Rural dwellers when driving into a city, often become somewhat confused. This is probably caused by information overload. Loud noises, bright colors, and many signs all contribute. The urban dweller adapts by rapidly filtering out almost all sensory input. When moving into the woods, they have to adjust to simplicity by turning the filters off.

Looking for subtle changes in the environment demands nearly total concentration by the tracker. The brain routes visual information through several different pathways. Not everything a searcher sees comes to consciousness.[1] More primitive parts of the brain, also involved in emotions, help determine what information reaches a state of consciousness. The greater the level of anxiety or emotional distraction, the less amount of visual information reaches consciousness.[2] Instead, the brain will focus on the one primary threat. Many readers have passed their eyes over the words in a book while they were upset or distracted, only to realize later they do not remember a word. Trackers recognize that they cannot track in an agitated or distracted state. They know that an agitated mind may be prone to failure but a relaxed mind, in tune with the environment, picks up the subtle clues. Many trackers appear to adopt Zen-like attitudes about tracking. While many non-trackers may snicker, the technique is well based in neurobiology.

Searchers also tend to *see* what they are interested in at that moment. For example, if they are thinking about having to go to work in a few hours, they may be allowing that thought to interfere with tracking. The best way to avoid distractions and emotional fear involves spending lots of quality time in the outdoor environment. Train, track by track and study the changing environment.

Search Awareness

The tracker constantly strives to increase awareness in order to increase the chances of visual recognition. At the very least, handlers must attempt not to distract the tracker. There are many situations that may affect a tracker's awareness on a search or when tracking. The following distractions are just a few of the possibilities and must be corrected as soon as they are recognized so that the searcher can devote his time and energy to tracking and searching.

Mental distractions may represent the greatest barrier to effective searching. Fear of the task, the night, or even of the lost subject, can make searching ineffective. Being apprehensive about the subject (which may be a good thing if he is armed), searching where assigned, or for any other reasons, are reasons to consider aborting the task. Unfortunately, law enforcement personnel may not have the luxury of aborting a task out of fear of harm to themselves.

Physical limitations must also be considered. Being cold, hot, tired, wet, or hungry can also have negative effects on tracking and searching effectiveness. Continuing to search under these conditions for the *good* of the missing person, may affect searching ability, causing harm to the searcher, team, or missing person. The tracker should know his limits and not push beyond them. The tracker and handler should also watch out for each other's safety. When both searchers are properly equipped, in good physical condition, and well trained much of this safety awareness can be refocused to searching.

Medical problems can also affect the searcher, team, and searching ability. Obesity, poor physical conditioning, heart disease, and other problems may distract attention from the assigned task.

Clustering up as a team often results during the night. When this happens, the team tends to talk to each other more often and about items unrelated to the search. This may decrease searching or tracking effectiveness. This also creates noise that could, and has, overridden the call of help from the missing person.

Some methods to reduce talking use hand signals or flashlights. These also keep the tracking personnel always on the alert, looking around and not locking into sign and tracks.

Shouting the lost person's name or blowing a whistle is a common search tactic. Many teams seem to focus on making noise and neglect techniques to increase auditory awareness. If calling out or whistling for the missing person, remember these tips.

- ✓ When calling stop the team. If the team tramps through the woods making noise in the leaves and underbrush, chances of hearing a weak response decrease tremendously. ˜

- ✓ Wait several moments (time is inexact) before beginning the task again after calling.

- ✓ Keep team members separated and not grouped up.

- ✓ Listen to the front, side, backwards, and upwards. Take time.

- ✓ The handler should pay attention to the canine. Look for any indications of an auditory alert.

Back at base, management faces many judgement calls. One family member emphatically reports the lost subject last wore sneakers while another one recalls work boots. Sometimes base may release both sets of information. In many regions it is more common for management to decide on the best information and then release that set to the field resources. Unfortunately this may result in releasing incorrect information. Utilizing this misinformation on tracking may also reduce awareness for the tracking person and canine handler. If base posts the missing person was wearing pink socks and the search teams just looks for those *pink* socks, they may miss other clues, sign, or tracks that are pertinent to the search. This holds true for all types of searchers; from the tracker to the handler's canine partner.

Visual Approach

Vision and analyzing are the most important aspects of tracking. The major problem appears to be that most searchers do not know how to see. Noted tracking instructor and artist Charles Worsham has observed the difference in visual strategies between the urban and natural environment.[3]

> Seeing in an urban setting usually consists of viewing complete whole objects and then moving to details to further refine, segregate and label. Seeing in nature, on the other hand, requires a form of vision which is more holistic, where we approach and enter the scene by getting a feel (*baselines*) for the overall landscape and the interrelationship of its elements. Then without looking for anything in particular, we should move on to search for small discordant visual cues which do not fit the overall pattern (*baselines again*). These visual cues will in turn lead to the discovery of whole objects which are hidden, obscured and fragmented by an environment which seeks to make everything in it less visible. [Italics added]

In our *everyday* lives we tend to look, and are taught to look, at or for the *whole* object before breaking it down into smaller pieces. Searchers should, in searching and tracking, be looking for the parts first, for if they do not, they may just miss the whole.

The authors are not preaching never look for the *track* (or the whole print). However, realize that most of the time all a tracking person or searcher may get is a disturbance from which to interpret or follow. If a tracker is looking for the parts, generally the whole will jump out at her, unless she is locked into only the parts and is not changing her vision or baselines. It is far too easy to miss the single lug of a boot, that made an impression in a quarter-sized area of soft soil, when looking for a mental picture of a complete footprint.

There is "...absolutely no doubt that an overwhelming majority of adults, way over 90 percent, cannot see except in the most primitive sense, such as identifying a neighbor's dog or traffic light."[4] Learning how to see also includes realizing that just because our *eyes* see something does not mean that our brain is interpreting what we are seeing correctly. In many of the author's tracking classes he has a student say, after having a subtle sign or disturbance pointed out, "Well, you can see it but I couldn't." This is not true. Each and every person (with some variances of course) can see *what* experienced trackers see. And they usually can see subtle signs once they have been pointed out. Experienced trackers have *taught* their brains to recognize and pay attention to visual information that most beginning tracking student's *file cabinets* (brain-memory) may be ignoring (see **Fig 3.1**). In their book *Inattentional Blindness*, authors Mack and Rock discuss how paying attention to the visual world affects seeing:

> How much, if anything, of our visual world do we perceive when we are not attending to it? ...Do we see (*sign and tracks*) because they have captured our attention or because our perception of them is independent of our attention?...Almost everyone at one time or another has had the experience of looking without seeing and of seeing what is not there. [5] [Italics added]

What Mack and Rock address, in a very scientific manner, is how the brain perceives the visual input it receives. When the brain has failed to learn to recognize what we are *looking* for, it may just ignore the information it is seeing. Generally, the brain strives to dominate what the eyes see and this may lead to false information. Continue to look at the whole, then the parts. When the brain begins to dominate, take a break and reassess. A tracker must train track-by-track, sign by sign, disturbance by disturbance and tear all signs and tracks apart to learn all the information they have to offer. This is the only way to become more proficient at tracking and signcutting and to be able to work effectively with a canine team.

Fig 3.1 *A picture of random spots? It may take a few seconds to see the image. However, once seen, it is impossible to miss and brain cells in the temporal lobe become altered permanently.[6] Trackers have taught their brains to recognize many subtle visuals changes such as shine, creases, rotated pebbles, and pressure releases, among others.*
Photo by Ron James

Trackers must vary their vision constantly looking forward, backward, to the sides, up and down. By using a 360 degree visual sweep, the tracker avoids locking in to one sign or track for too long. More distant sign and tracks can be strung together. When the daytime conditions are right or at night (utilizing lights, angles, and tactics correctly) sometimes a searcher may be able to see the *tracks* fifty yards or more in front of them. This may be the most important tactic for the tracker working with the fast-moving canine team.

One final note on vision. Searchers should not allow their eyes to jump around. Searchers "searching" the woods or a dirt road generally move their eyes in a sporadic manner. This is natural. But an effective tracker looks at larger objects, then slows eye movement down, and starts *caressing* the environment slowly, being certain to systemically look into the negative spaces.

> **You see what you know or think you know;**
> **the trick is to know what you see.** –Charles Worsham[7]

This technique is taught by the Coast Guard and Civil Air Patrol to the observers who fly on aerial search missions.[8] Unfortunately, many ground searchers just look from tree to tree.

Increasing Search Awareness Tips

- Relax — take deep breaths — exhale quickly.
- Clear the mind as much as possible. There will always be unwanted information that will come into consciousness when trying to search. This is natural. Allow those thoughts to come and then go. Turn down the volume.
- As mentioned several times in this book, keep talking at a minimum. Talking or even listening to talk can negatively affect awareness. Communication with team members should be in a quiet voice.
- Always establish baselines.
- Don't **lock-in** to only one tactic.
- Let go of time. Don't look at a watch every few minutes to see how much longer the task is going to last. Sometimes base may assign a task that they say should take two hours, but in reality will take four to six hours. Be patient. It is better to do a comprehensive partial task than an incomplete whole one.
- Don't lock-in for any length of time. Falling in love with a track will quickly burn a tracker out, especially at night, and will affect awareness.
- Take breaks *before* they are needed. Sit down and relax the mind, eyes, and body.
- Practice and become competent working with a canine team at the speeds they may operate.
- Do not ignore intuition. Intuition comes in many forms for many reasons. Remember to recognize when something is trying to get your attention and listen to it.

Tracking Tactics

Before a tracker can follow a set of tracks they must first find one. Looking for sign (such as a creased leaf), clues, disturbances, or tracks is often called signcutting. The tracker will use a special set of tactics when signcutting for the elusive first track/sign. Once they have located the trail, they may use several different tactics to follow it to the subject. The following is not intended to represent an exhaustive list of all tactics. Many of these tactics require two or more teams of trackers. Obviously, when working in a combined tracker/dog handler team, the tracker may not be able to use all of these tactics. However, it is important for the handler to realize the capabilities of the experienced tracker.

Expanding Circle Signcutting. The expanding circle is used to originally locate clues, signs, and tracks. The tactic is most commonly used at the PLS, LKP, from a located clue, or any other suspected sign area. When the tracker is unable to find the track the tracker signcuts in circles expanding outward for a distance determined by the conditions and terrain. This tactic is especially useful in trashed areas. When starting at the PLS, the tracker knows each circle does in fact intersect at some point with the track. Once a track is located, the tracker switches to track-by-track in order to determine the direction of travel.

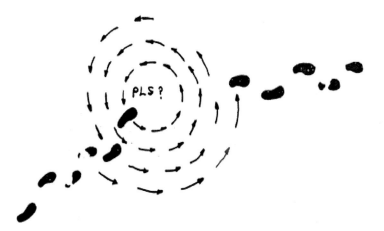

Fig 3.2 *Expanding circle signcutting. The tracker starts at the PLS and signcuts in an ever expanding circle in order to locate sign.*

Track-by-Track. Track-by-track represents the most basic tracking tactic. All tracking students begin and continue their career by practicing track-by-track. It forces the student to find the next track even when it is difficult to locate. In order to facilitate finding the next track, the tracker will look at the ground at several different angles, shine flashlights or use mirrors to bring out shadows, and might use a tape measure or tracking stick. Track-by-track is the only tactic that allows the tracker to definitively state the trail belongs to the missing subject. Students, even when they see a possible track 10 feet ahead, must still find every track. For this reason, track-by-track takes considerable time and cannot catch a moving subject.

Leap Frogging. Trackers developed leap frogging in order to overcome the significant time required by track-by-track. The tactic generally requires two teams of trackers. The leaping involves moving from the known tracks to find another set. The leap can be anywhere from 10 yards to 100 yards depending upon the terrain conditions. Ideally, a second team or tracker works track-by-track from the leap point to confirm the two trails connect.

Fig. 3.3 *Leap frogging. Tracker A starts at the original set of tracks. Tracker B then leaps over A an appropriate distance and finds the next tracks. Once Tracker B has found and confirmed the measurements, Tracker A leaps over B and repeats the process.*

Accordion Tracking. Trackers deploy the accordion tactic under similar circumstances as leap frogging. It requires at least two trackers. While in leap frogging the team members pass each other, in accordion tracking the teams do not. This may be the more appropriate tactics when the lead tracker is more skilled at finding sign.

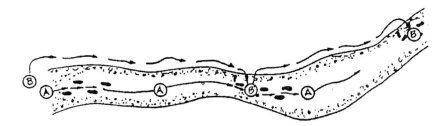

Fig 3.4 *In Accordion tracking, Tracker B jumps to find the next trap. When Tracker B leaps again, Tracker A moves up to Tracker B's last location and starts track-by-track.*

Collapsing Circle Signcutting. The collapsing circle tactic is a signcutting tactic best used to determine if a subject has left a defined area. Frequently, the location of the PLS is not always precise. Instead, information only suggests a general location the subject was last seen. In these cases, the tracker typically begins by signcutting perimeters and features. Each subsequent pass tightens the circle around a target.

Zig-Zag Signcutting. Zig-Zag signcutting's goal is to locate tracks within a specific area with defined borders (see **Fig 3.5**). In many cases the tracker may choose to signcut the perimeter first. The pattern is similar to the grid pattern used by air-scent dog handlers.

Perimeter Signcutting. Perimeter is often an assigned tactic by management to trackers or may be incorporated when given a specific area. The goals of a perimeter search include locating clues, signs, tracks, possible turnoffs, and determining if the subject moved through the area. Perimeters often include features such as trails, roads, and streams that are good for tracking (see **Fig 3.5**).

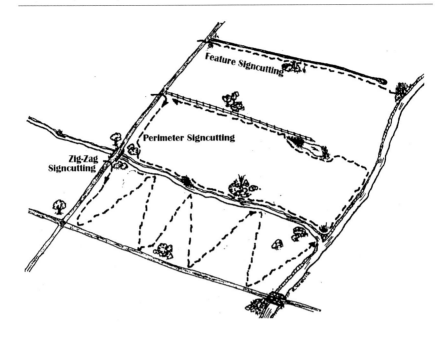

Fig 3.5 *The signcutting tactics of zig-zag, perimeter, and feature demonstrated in three different search areas.*

Feature Signcutting. Signcutting a feature such as a road, trail, creek, or gully offers the opportunity to find excellent **track traps**. In addition, these types of features often attract lost subjects. Among dog handlers and ground searchers this is often called a hasty search (see **Fig 3.5**).

1. Ramachandran, V., Blakeslee, S. (1998) *Phantoms in the Brain.* William Morrow and Company. NY, NY.

2. Goleman, D. (1995) *Emotional Intelligence.* Bantam. NY, NY.

3. Worsham, C. (1999) *Techniques of Tracking on Various Ground Covers.* Madison Hgts, VA.

4. Nelson, G, (1977) *How to See: A guide to reading our man made environment*, Little, Brown & Co. Boston, MA.

5. Mack, A., Rock, I., (1998) *Inattentional Blindness*, Massachusetts Institute of Technology, Boston, MA.

6. Tovee, M., Rolls, E., Ramachandran, V. (1996) Rapid Visual Learning in Neurons in the Primate Visual Cortex. *Neuroreport*, Vol 7

7. Worsham, C. (1996) *Locating Tracks-Visual Perception and the File Cabinet.* Madison Hgts.

8. Interagency Committee on Search and Rescue (1991) National Search and Rescue Manual Volume I: National Search and Rescue System. Joint Pub 3-50, COMDTINST M16120.5A

4. Search Dog Resources & Tactics

Search Dog Types

Three basic types of trained dogs exist that work in SAR missions. The definitions listed below may not be universally accepted by the canine community, but are the terms that are used by accepted SAR textbooks.[1] Thus, anyone not familiar with the terminology used in their area to classify canine teams should check with a knowledgeable local source.

Air-scent Dogs. These dogs work primarily off lead to locate sources of human scent, much like a pointer or setter in the hunting environment. The dogs, with training, identify and follow airborne human scent. Many of the SAR dog units in the country train their dogs to locate the source of any human scent, not just the scent of the subject. As a result, these handlers will not be interested in a scent article from the subject. Also, as a result of this type of training, these dogs may locate other people that happen to be in the assigned search area. In most cases this is not a significant hindrance to effective performance and can actually be of benefit in certain scenarios. However, it does mean that this type of dog team cannot effectively work an area that has also been assigned to other types of resources without careful planning and coordination.

Some air-scent dog units or handlers may also train their air-scent dogs for scent-discrimination. That is, the dog will try to locate only the scent of a particular person. These dog handlers will frequently ask for scent articles. Thus, these teams may be able to work areas concurrently with other resources. They may also be more efficient for searching in contaminated areas in urban or suburban search scenarios or in areas that cannot be reasonably evacuated such as nursing homes, manufacturing operations, and airport terminal areas. That is not meant to imply, however, that properly trained non-scent discriminating air-scent dogs cannot be used to search those types of areas.

While all air-scent dogs should show interest in the scent emanating from articles left behind by individuals, there are some considerable differences of opinion among handlers as to whether the dogs should be trained to indicate articles. As a result, even within a single SAR unit, some dogs may be trained to indicate articles while others are not.

Air-scent dogs do not rely on starting on or discovering the actual path walked by a subject. Therefore, they are able to effectively search arbitrary areas for the subject and can efficiently conduct search operations when a useful PLS or LKP is not available.

Tracking Dogs. These dogs are often referred to as "hot track" dogs. Many police K-9 dogs fall into this category. These dogs are trained essentially to follow the scent of the last person to pass through an area. They are not generally trained to start from a scent article, but can frequently be started from the scent in a car that a person has left behind (as long as the car has not been contaminated by the scent of others). As with any class of search dog, the individual dog's capabilities will depend heavily on the types of training that the handler does with it. Some of these dogs may be very good at following a track that has had other, fresher tracks laid across or beside it. While many tracking dogs may be diverted by the fresher tracks.

Many times a tracking dog will be the first available canine asset on the scene because of the wide use of such dogs in the law enforcement community. Even if they are not able to track all the way to the missing subject, tracks identified by these dogs can establish direction of travel or potentially provide other critical insight into the missing person scenario. Because of their law enforcement use, many of the handlers have no need to train their dogs on tracks with age characteristics of those encountered in the search and rescue community. Thus, many of these dogs will not be of much value in search operations where the PLS/LKP is days old. Again, that is completely dependent on the training of the individual handler and dog. Individual handlers should be consulted on the dog's actual training and capabilities.

Trailing dogs. These dogs are frequently referred to as scent-discriminating dogs. They are trained to start from a scent article, or possibly from an uncontaminated footprint, and follow the scent trail left by only that specific individual. In some parts of the country, because most of the scent-discriminating trailing dogs are **bloodhounds**, SAR personnel may refer to this class of dogs as simply "bloodhounds." That terminology can be misleading because not all bloodhounds are properly trained and tested, and because other breeds of dogs can also be trained to do scent-discrimination trailing.

The scent-discriminating ability of the trailing dog gives those teams the capability to do several things that a tracking dog team cannot do. In order to do these things, they will, of course, need appropriate scent articles to start the dog. First of all, they can usually establish a track from a PLS/LKP that has been contaminated beyond the point of usefulness to a tracking dog. They can also generally follow older, more contaminated tracks than the tracking dog. Many can be used to confirm whether or not tracks or clues found by other teams were left by the subject. Since the scent may be dispersed by the wind or collect in nearby foliage, the trailing dog may not follow in the exact footsteps of the subject. This may allow the tracker to follow on a trail while the handler and dog are fighting through brush just a few feet away. In addition to following the trail left by an individual, trailing dogs that have been trained to **cast** for the start of a track over large areas can be used for binary search tactics. The team can provide confirmation that the subject did not pass a specific boundary, such as a road, stream bed, fence line, etc., or, if they establish a track while casting along such a boundary, they have contributed to identification of a new LKP.

Since many of the trailing dog handlers are also from the law enforcement community, in many cases the dogs have been trained only for the type of cases that the handler is generally involved with. Therefore, even with scent-discriminating trailing dogs, it is important for search management to ascertain from the individual handlers the types of training that have been done and the types of cases that the dog team is generally involved with.

There are other characteristics which define the differences between tracking and trailing dogs, but that is beyond the scope of this text. Both types of dogs can be of great value to search operations when properly employed by knowledgeable search management.

Tactics

There are several different tactics that air-scent dog handlers may use to search their assigned areas. The choice of tactics is dependent on such things as weather, wind direction, terrain, vegetation, subject characteristics, desired POD, the dog's searching characteristics, previous efforts in the sector, handler preferences, how tired the dog and handler are, and numerous other factors. As a result, it is unlikely that any two handlers would work a search area in exactly the same way.

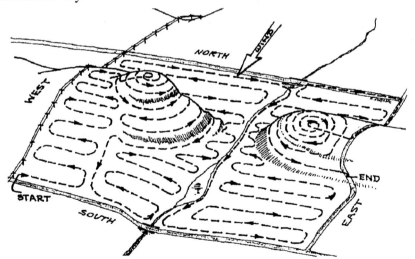

Fig 4.1 *A dog team assigned to "grid" a sector chooses to use a variety of tactics. They grid the open areas, contour the hills, and do a hasty search down the creek.*[2]

The tactics handlers choose from consist of **hasty**, **contour**, or **grid** tactics. While there is some overlap in definitions, when used to describe sector search tactics these terms frequently have different interpretations than when used from a task-definition perspective.[2] For example, a dog team may be assigned a hasty task by search management to search a streambed. Once in the field, however, the handler may chose to use a modified form of contouring as the best method for performing a systematic search of the stream bed **(Fig 4.2)**. Or, when given an area search assignment by the search management, the handler may chose to use hasty search techniques to cover the sector if there are numerous logging roads or trails in the assigned area. More likely than not, the tactics chosen by the handler to cover the assigned search area will be some combination of all of the available tactics as the team adapts to the terrain and changing wind conditions.

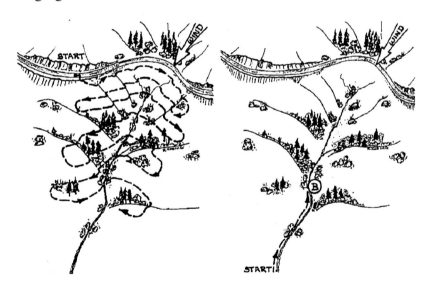

Fig 4.2 *Handler A (left) is using contouring to achieve a higher POD for the entire drainage, while Handler B (right) has chosen to follow the creek in a more classic "hasty" pattern.*

Alerts and Indications

In the terminology used here, **alert** refers to the observable changes in an air-scenting dog's focus, intensity, and body language that indicate it has detected human scent. It is an untrained behavior, but one that every dog handler should be familiar with, and be able to describe for her dog. This is contrary to the definition used in some parts of the country and on many of the FEMA Urban SAR teams. In those cases, alert is used to refer to the trained **indication** that the dog uses to demonstrate to the handler that he has found a person (or, perhaps, an article). In our terminology, that part of the behavior chain is refered to as the indication.

When an air-scenting dog is working a search task, there is generally a very marked change in the observable behavior of the dog when it detects human scent. In most cases, the head will go up and/or out as if reaching or stretching for the scent; the intensity, focus, and pace of the dog usually change dramatically; dogs such as German shepherds may raise both their tails and ears as they focus on following the scent. The dog will obviously be trying to locate the source of the scent.

When an air-scenting dog is working a search task, there is generally a very marked change in the observable behavior of the dog when it detects human scent. In most cases, the head will go up and/or out as if reaching or stretching for the scent; the intensity, focus, and pace of the dog usually change dramatically; dogs such as German shepherds may raise both their tails and ears as they focus on following the scent. The dog will obviously be trying to locate the source of the scent. The motion of the dog may be linear as if it is going directly to the scent source, or it may be a back and forth coning motion as the dog works to define the extent and gradient of the scent field.

Frequently handlers will differentiate the strength of the alerts by defining them as strong (or hard or intense), and weak (or soft). A soft, or weak, alert is an alert in which the dog briefly shows heightened interest in following a scent, but does not follow it far or long. Such an alert usually does not last more than a few seconds and does not cause the dog to deviate much from its original path. On hard, or strong, alerts the dog may stay focused on working out the source of the scent for a number of minutes, and may lead the team hundreds of yards from the spot at which it picked up the scent.

The location of alerts, time of the alerts, and wind directions should be noted on the map of the search sector. Some strong alerts may be reported immediately to base so that follow up actions may be taken. On the other hand, the handler may chose not to report all of the **weak alerts** observed by the team while on the task.

There are two principal behavior chains used in the air-scent search dog community. One method teaches the dog to stay with the subject once it has made a find, and bark until the handler and other team members arrive at that location.

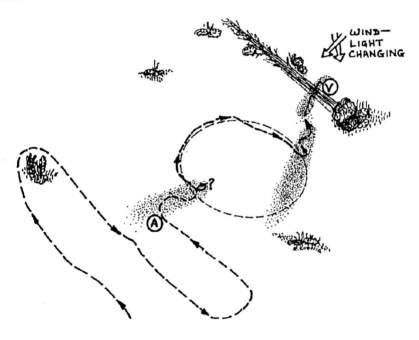

Fig 4.3 *Variable winds. In conditions of light changing winds it is common for a dog to alert and then lose the scent.[2]*

The other method of training teaches the dog to return to the handler after making a find; give the handler some positive indication that a person, or object has been found; and then lead the handler back to the subject. The first methodology is frequently referred to as the **bark indication** or **bark alert** method. The second type is generally referred to as the **find-refind** method.

The bark indication sequence has essentially already been defined. The dog detects scent, follows it into the subject, and starts barking until the handler arrives. In the find-refind sequence, the dog detects scent, follows it into the subject, returns to the handler, provides the handler with some indication that it has made a find, and then leads the handler back to the subject. The indication in the find-refind sequence may take a number of forms. Some dog handlers may just rely on reading the dog's body language, while others may train their dogs to bark, sit, jump, pull at a tug attached to the handler's belt, or pick up a **bringsel**. A bringsel is usually something like a leather strap hanging from the dog's collar. After making the find, the dog will pick the bringsel up and hold it in its mouth while returning to the handler.

Each type of indication has advantages and disadvantages. A bark indication may not be heard if the dog locates the subject at a very great range from the search team, if the team is working in a noisy environment, or if the team is busy breaking a trail through dense vegetation. A handler extricating himself from a briar thicket might not see his dog return and sit to give an indication. Numerous situations exist for which each method of training has some shortcomings.

1. LaValla, R., Stoffel, S., Jones, T. (1997) *Search Is An Emergency: A text for managing search operations* (4th Ed). Emergency Response Institute. Olympia, Washington.

2. Koenig, M. (1993) Wilderness Search Strategy for Dog Handlers. *NASAR Conference Proceedings*. NASAR. Chantilly, ViA

5. Tracker-Handler Guidelines

The tracker should ask the handler what the canine team expects from the tracker.

The canine handlers should explain where they want the tracker to walk in relationship to the handler and the dog. Procedures should be discussed concerning actions to take if the dog alerts and/or follows scent away from planned route, or if the tracker identifies notable sign. The team must resolve task delegation such as communication and navigation.

The tracker should inform the handler of his tracking skills.

Trackers should exchange information on what tracking training and certifications they have. They should also state any previous experiences working with dog teams. Both members should briefly discuss law enforcement background, rescue/medical training, land navigation, and communication background.

The handler and tracker need to briefly exchange information on procedures and general requirements for tracking and dog handling.

The discussion should include such topics as types of track traps, how the tracker looks for track traps, how track traps are utilized after they have been identified, and how the tracker will be looking for signs of passage and clues. The tracker should point out the importance of the dog handler controlling the dog to keep them off a track the tracker is examining. The dog handler should address such topics as search tactics (general patterns), how alerts are followed up, how the dog alerts and indicates, the pace the dog works, how often breaks are taken, and whether interrupting a task will interfere with the dog. Both handlers and trackers may have to make slight modifications to normal procedures in order to best work together. No resource is better than another, just different. Work as a team!

Inquire if the canine handler has any tracking training.

If so, discuss how the handler uses this training on tasks. Inquire about the type and source of training.

Request the handler to take breaks near track traps so the tracker can signcut the area.

This may be the tracker's only chance, depending on training and tracking expertise level, to effectively signcut/track.

Inform team members of any medical problems.

Discuss among team members allergies (bee stings-anaphylactic shock), diabetes, heart problems, relevant medications, etc. Make sure the team leader or medic knows where team members medications are carried, if applicable.

The handler should explain how his dog alerts.

When assigned to a task with an air-scent dog team, tracking personnel should ask the dog handler to describe how their dog alerts and indicates. Some canine teams work and alert differently. While performing the search task, tracking personnel may observe something in the dog's behavior that the handler does not. The tracker using scanning tactics may pick up on an alert. In the search environment, having a second set of eyes and ears observing the dog, and possibly listening for barking, can be crucial to search success. Tracking personnel can be of significant benefit if they watch, or listen for, the dog while the dog handler is performing some action that would inhibit his seeing an alert or indication, or hearing a bark indication. The tracker should pass any relevant observation on to the handler. See Chapter Four for more information on alerts and indications.

Touch or talk to the dog only after obtaining the handler's permission or if there is an immediate danger to the dog.

The handler should explain what to expect from the dog in response to touching or grabbing the dog if the need should arise.

While on the Task

Keep the task safe.

Do not exceed training and expertise. Know personal limits and stay within them.

If the tracker finds a prime track area...

inform the handler. If the canine team cannot stop its task at that time, mark the area on the map and flag it. Then catch up with the canine team. At the next available opportunity determine an appropriate response with the team leader. That response could include returning to the track area or informing base. Base will log the area then plan appropriate follow up. The reporting team may be requested to return to the track.

Different tactics and approaches may by used by handlers within the same area.

Be aware that scent-discriminating dogs, as with air-scent dogs, may use the same or totally different tactics, even within the same area. Two air-scent dogs may work the same task differently.

Follow the handler's directives about where the tracker should work in relation to the handler and the dog.

Generally the tracker will be asked to stay behind or to the downwind side of the canine team. This may vary within the task. The location chosen by the handler is based upon wind currents and the scent cone in order to minimize scent contamination. Different dogs range at varying distances depending on terrain, wind, training, and the dog's experience.

Be aware that search dogs may go where the scent takes them.

Generally, once the dog detects scent, the team will follow the dog regardless of assigned area or terrain. Teams have often been lead through thick foliage. If the dog leads the team out of its assigned area, the teams position should be reported to base. When working with scent-discriminating dogs the scent may be well off the trail, requiring the team to move through thick vegetation.

Some handlers will not want to break their dog's concentration during a task.

Tracking and trailing dogs may not be willing to stop while actively working a scent trail. Most have trained to stop and start if required. But, in reality handlers do not like stopping their dog once on a trail. However, the handler should make every effort to avoid walking through track-traps. The tracker, since he is following the potential trail, should make attempts to signcut on the fly. If the tracking/ trailing dog does take a break or stops at a scent pool the tracker should take the opportunity to verify the track. The tracker must be careful not to disturb the trail where the dog was stopped, especially the area the dog has not yet covered. Therefore, it is important that the tracker-handler closely coordinate activities during breaks.

Air-scent dogs generally work longer tasks and take periodic breaks during those tasks. Regardless of the specifics of the dog's training, very few, if any, handlers will be willing to stop their dogs while they are alerting so that the tracker can pursue other clues. However, since many air-scent dogs will alert and attempt to follow trails left behind by an individual even though they may not be trained to track, the point at which the dog loses the track should be a good opportunity for the handler to rest the dog and for the tracker to look for sign. Some handlers will be able to tell when their dogs are alerting on tracks. Others may not be able to. However, before taking a break and permitting the tracker to signcut, the handler will probably work an area around the point at which the dog lost the track or return to the starting point in an attempt to pick the scent up again.

Critical alerts of where the dog lost the scent have been discounted by handlers on actual searches because they knew that other search personnel had recently passed through their assigned area near that location. On other searches, inexperienced handlers have spent hours chasing the residual scent of the sweep team that had just completed searching the same area. Skilled trackers can provide critical data for making tactical decisions in the field.

Canine teams work at different speeds.

The speeds are determined by the pace of the dog. If the tracker slows them down, they may lose their efficiency. Some dogs lose their concentration if their pace is drastically changed.

Keep talking to a minimum.

Both the tracking person and the handler should be talking as little as possible. Not only might talking interfere with the canine team, it also interferes with tracking baselines. Try to get as much information before the task begins or wait until the end of the task to ask general questions. In the case of an emergency or seeing important clues, it may be necessary to say something. Common sense must prevail.

Maintain the proper distance between the tracker, handler, and dog.

It is important for the tracker to adhere to the handler's instructions on where the tracker should be in relation to the dog while the dog is working. The handler should not only specify a direction, "stay to my left and slightly behind me," but also a distance, "please try to stay within 25 feet of me." The distance will vary based on the dog, terrain, and wind conditions in the assigned search area. Many dogs will judge who is on the team by the distance separating the various individuals from the handler. As a result, a team member outside of that range, such as a tracker who frequently lags behind while checking sign, may be a constant distraction for the dog. If the tracker lags, the air-scent dog may interpret the reduced scent as a find. In unsteady wind conditions, the scent coming from a widely separated team member may be confused with the weak scent coming from a victim. This may cause the dog to fail to alert on the desired target. In addition, a tracker that regularly diverts from the primary path of travel without informing the dog handler will distract the handler.

The tracker should also avoid working too close to the handler. This will interfere with the tracker's visual searching. It also increases the chances of lights being accidentally shined into the tracker's eyes.

Since many trackers utilize hand signals for distance communication, it may be possible to set up some simple protocols with the dog handler. However, the tracker must realize that since the handler is generally quite busy watching the dog, navigating, and also conducting visual searching, looking for hand signals may overwhelm the handler.

Maintain proper team orientation.

Trackers are trained to usually work in front of teams. However, when management combines a tracker with a canine team the purpose is usually for the tracker to augment the canine. Moving in front of the canine may disrupt or destroy the normal function of the dog. This is particularly true of trailing/tracking dogs. However, significant opportunities for the skills of the tracker to be used still exist. Trailing dogs often work downwind from the actual trail of the subject. This provides the chance for the tracker to work an undisturbed track along a trail while the handler struggles through briars. When an air-scent dog handler works features such as power-line cuts, logging, woods, roads, or trails where a dense border of foliage exists along the boundary, the dog team often makes passes along both sides. Thus, by coordinating with the handler, it may be possible for the tracker to work the primary feature (power-line cut, road, trail) while the dog team covers the area upwind and on the other side of the foliage boundary.

Avoid slowing down the canine team.

The tracker will not be able to stop and look at everything. The tracker must know their expertise levels and stay within them. Trackers should practice tracking at increased speeds. Experience has shown that tracking personnel are able to detect sign at the increased speeds.

Do not wander off!

Its important to work together as a team. If the team becomes separated, a team member may be left behind or become lost. In either case team safety has been compromised, operational protocols broken, search resources needlessly diverted from finding the subject, and teammates will tease the lost team member for several years.

Don't shoot from the hip.

Dog handlers or trackers who makes statements, judgments, or calls beyond their skill and experience level could ruin their reputation for years. It is best to present facts and observations to base. Any interpretation of the facts must be clearly explained as such.

The team leader is in charge of the team.

Team members must follow directions. Do not get into arguments in the field. If a team member does not follow directions, the leader may send him back to base and request not to work with him again.

Always act with professionalism.

6. Tracking Misconceptions

Many searcher's and law enforcement personnel's first contact with tracking is through television, movies, books, etc. In many cases they have formed many preconceived ideas about tracking. This chapter will assist in a better understanding of tracking. The following illustrate but a few of the many uninformed comments uttered from non-tracking personnel, tracking students, and even tracking personnel over the years.

"The only people that were skillful at tracking were the Native Americans."

This idea has been instilled into the understanding of tracking for centuries. One must always remember that probably *all* of us have ancestors that came from a society that relied upon tracking for their existence (the hunter-gatherers).

Very little is written about tracking by Native Americans. What is written tends to only address tracking in a mystical fashion. The material lacks a how-to approach.

The major difference between the present and the past is that most current societies do not need tracking in their everyday life. Finding a food source is more likely to involve a search for car keys and wallet than the track of an elusive rabbit.

Tracking has become specialized over the years: search and rescue, law enforcement, military, animal tracking, forensic studies, the analysis of dinosaur tracks, and recreational tracking are just a few of the specialties. Over the past 10-20 years, there has been an increased interest in traditional tracking.

The authors believe that a person can, indeed, learn something about tracking from a one-hour, quality tracking lecture. In many of the lectures, the student will receive information useful to them in the field or base. More information and quality tracking schools are available than ever before.[1] Even though no one may ever achieve the levels of our ancestors, the tools to assist the student exist and people still have the ability.

"Tracking and signcutting can only work if the PLS, LKP (or crime scene) has not been trashed or contaminated."

As a large portion of the tracking and law enforcement community knows, most PLS and LKPs are trashed or contaminated before their arrival. This is a problem that most tracking personnel have faced. It is particularly common in areas that are not receptive to the skills associated with tracking or in areas that believe tracking can only be useful under certain misunderstood conditions. This problem is exacerbated by not having enough suitably trained tracking resources available to respond in a timely manner.

There are always going to be complicating conditions and problems normally associated with the beginning of a SAR mission. First the family searches, then the family's friends may join in the search. Later the local law enforcement agency, local fire departments, local rescue squads, and local volunteers may be called for the search. Only much later may a request for *professional* search resources occur. In many of these **incidents**, local resources find the missing subject.

Crime scenes also sometimes become compromised. The priorities of a police officer arriving on scene are safety and   protection of life and property. They may not have the training, awareness, time, or ability to observe where they or others on scene have walked. It some areas, when a law enforcement officer discovers that they have responded to what appears to be a *search* for a missing person instead of a *crime*, they may forget their training or disregard the role of the first responder. The first responder must always protect the PLS or LKP. This is why every PLS or LKP should ideally be treated as a crime scene.

Even though a PLS or LKP has been trashed, it still should be *signcut* by a competent tracking person if possible. Management should request that any *tracker*-checked area be checked again by another tracking person. It is very possible that the first team that checked an area could have missed the one sign or track that could assist the search. The PLS task should always be repeated if possible. If the area is trashed beyond hope, a tracking person may still use many other tactics.

In most parts of the country the tracking person's job is not so much to *find* the missing person tracks but to evaluate clues (especially footprints) that have been found by other teams. Other common tasks involve *eliminating* areas. Many tracking personnel are assigned areas to determine whether a person has passed through them. These areas are often trails, roads, ravines, and other search sectors. If the tracker is proficient this could eliminate this area and redirect the search effort to other areas. The tracker may also be called to check out clues that have been called into base. These may include sign, clothing, tracks, or beddings. This can lead to either a positive identification (as much as positive as possible) that the clue belongs to the missing person or redirecting the search to another sector. With most significant clues, a canine team is sent to follow up.

"A tracking person is required to follow the tracks, track-by-track."

Most of the tracking literature states that the tracker must have a known track to start from and follow. To do otherwise, it states, is incompetent.

Even though this method can certainly be useful (especially in training and learning how to see tracks and sign) and has led to many finds, at most searches time is of the essence. The luxury of following known tracks can be, at best, very time consuming. This is why signcutting and tracking tactics were developed. This is also why management often dispatches canine teams into the field.

> **Caution:** Leaving or getting in front of the last known track may destroy further signs and track. Choose carefully which tracks should be used and how to approach other areas. The preferred approach is the path of *greatest resistance*.

Depending on the tracking resources available, other tactics may include leap frogging, inchworming, cross tracking, and zig-zag tracking. In each case it is advisable, if not required, to leave a tracking team member at the last known track (at the least, this sign or track needs to be marked so that it can be found later by the current team or another team). This person should follow the track, track-by-track, until notified by team members signcutting or tracking ahead that they have found other tracks or sign that they can relate to the missing person or can string together with the last known track.

"A clue (personal item from the missing person) has no meaning to the tracking person."

Every clue has the potential of holding great operational significance to all field resources. This is why it is important to have base personnel, especially the operations section staff, trained in the foundations of tracking. They are in the position to evaluate the relevance and importance of clues, signs, and tracks located by field resources. More importantly, it is the operations section that will direct the immediate follow up response to reported clues. This response may include the deployment of trackers, trailing dogs, air-scent dogs, or a combination team. Another alternative to an entire staff trained to properly evaluate tracking clues is to have a base sign-cutting/tracking coordinator available.

A frequent problem occurs when a field team reports finding a clue, sign, or track. Now someone must determine whether or not that clue has any relevance to the search. A skilled tracker examining the physical clue can signcut the area, find more tracks, and determine a direction of travel. Careful examination of the tracks can help establish if the subject left the clue.

Another possible response to a reported physical clue is to deploy a scent-discriminating dog to the site of the clue to help verify the clue and potentially establish a track and direction of travel. Since the tracker will also attempt to determine a possible track and direction of travel from a *clue*, integrating the two resources, if possible, makes sense.

"A known shoe size equals a certain (exact) shoe length."

This statement has probably created more problems at base and in the field than any other. There are charts available to the searcher and base that equates a shoe size to an exact shoe length.[2] Do not put a lot of value on these charts. Newer research suggests these charts are no longer valid.

In the past, there was much more correlation between shoe sizes and length. Today, the market is inundated with so many **outsole** patterns, shapes, and designs that even the FBI's shoe print database has a difficult time keeping up with the new models now being placed on the market.[3]

Another problem is that about 90% of the shoes sold in North America are manufactured in other countries. This, creates problems because of differences in manufacturing processes, different manufacturers, and the lack of strict quality control of shoes that are the same model. Just one model could be made in several differently owned factories from several different countries.

A shoe size does not relate to an exact shoe length! Only a range of lengths may be applicable (may differ up to two inches). The following practical experiment demonstrates the range of shoe lengths for one person.

> **Practical Experiment**
> 1. Gather all of the shoes you own.
> 2. Determine the measurements of each shoe.

Today, people have many different type of shoes: dress, walking, running, hiking, mountaineering, casual, boat casuals, etc. Problems arise when a missing person's family member produces a shoe that belongs to the missing person. This shoe is a size 9 sneaker. The missing person is reported to be wearing hiking shoes. There could be several inches difference in the measurements between these two shoes.

In the 1980's, Michael J. Cassidy of the Royal Canadian Mounted Police conducted a study.[4] He utilized four different types of footwear: welted boots with a normal heel, work boots/snow boots, cowboy boots, and running shoes/flat bottom casuals. The study showed that an impression measurement of 12 inches could have a difference of 2½ shoe sizes. He concluded that shoe sizes vary in length and widths, and shoe sizes don't relate to an exact shoe lengths. Depending on the type of shoe, the manufacturing process, or the outsole material, a shoe size can vary as much as 2.5 inches.

"When lacking the missing subject's shoe print just go to the store and buy the same shoe."

Just because a family member purchases another shoe that is the exact shoe the family states the missing person was wearing does not mean that shoe has the exact same outsole pattern, shape, or measurements. Same shoe models may have different outsole patterns/designs.

"Specific types of shoes always have a distinctive outsole pattern."

Dress shoes (the days of the tracking person relying upon a dress shoe having a flat outsole are now history), western boots, and sneakers now may have lug sole patterns. Docker/boat type casual shoes also have many different outsole designs and patterns.

"A person's height is related to their shoe size."

A person's height cannot be accurately related to that person's shoe size, according to the studies done by Cassidy and Bodziak. Bodziak cites a height calculation chart from Cassidy that shows that a male with a shoe size of 9½ could have a height ranging from 5'8" to 6'. The study also cites a survey of 399 male shoe sizes, which found that 6'1" males had shoe sizes that ranged from 8½ to 13.[3,4]

"A person's stride is related to their height."

A person's stride can't be accurately related to that person's height. Cassidy's study once again showed great variability between height and stride. The relatively small sample size of eight 5'11" males demonstrated strides ranging from 24" to 33.5". This represents almost a 40% increase from the shortest stride to the longest.[4]

Management's Dilemma

Trackers hunger for information. Their great need for the mental image of what the subject's footprint looks like can lead to *lock-in*. They also thirst for accurate subject measurements. Base personnel, in an attempt to satisfy these critical needs, will often resort to some of the common pitfalls; estimating size from other shoes, purchasing the "identical shoe model," or guessing pattern from shoe type. If any of this information is collected by base, it should, most of the time, remain at base. The average searcher tends to *lock* into any description given to them, which may cause him to look only for that information and not to look for anything else. In other words, they could overlook the real track or sign because a track or sign that they may have found does not *match* the one given to them. These observations are based upon critical errors that have occurred on search incidents.

However, all information should be given to experienced tracking personnel. Tracking personnel will utilize this information correctly and will not lock into it. If a searcher finds a track that may match the description that base has, then a red flag should go up and more investigation is needed. As with all clues, the origin and dependability of footwear information should be questioned.

"Tracking personnel need a shoe (pair of shoes) that belongs to the missing person so that they may record the wear patterns, size, length, etc. They will utilize this information to match up tracks that may be found in the field."

Some tracking personnel will not leave base until they have a shoe that belongs to the missing person to record measurements and wear patterns from. Even though this *shoe* could give a tracking person guidelines to operate from, they must be used with caution (see the "management's dilemma" sidebar).

"Tracking and signcutting can't be done at night."

The most common reasons given to tracking personnel and searchers by either base operations or the responsible agent (RA) for shutting down ground search operations at nightfall or failing to initiate a ground search until daybreak are: 1) searching at night is too dangerous; 2) searching at night is useless; and 3) searchers are not prepared to search at night. While these concerns are valid in some situations, trained searchers and especially trained trackers may even prefer to track at night.

1) *"Searching at night is too dangerous."*

Current and future weather conditions, the terrain where the search team has been assigned, the searcher's previous training and experience, and on-site personnel and equipment prepared-ness must be taken into account when deciding whether to search at night. The possibility that the searcher(s) could be placed into personal jeopardy and risk (whether real or imagined) from local inhabitants, criminals, or even the missing person must also be considered. However, night itself should not be a concern to trained searchers. The possibility of walking off a drop-off and branches snapping back into searchers' eyes are the chief concerns. All of these concerns exist during the daylight hours. However, these concerns are increased at night. The night searchers should have training and experience at night.

2) *"Searching at night is useless."*

This comment usually comes from someone without training or experience in night searching (tracking and signcutting). While it is true that the POD for grid/sweep searches will be reduced when searching for an immobile, unresponsive subject, the same cannot be said for tracking and canine resources. Since it is easier to hear during the night it is often easier to find a mobile or responsive subject. Tracking, trailing, and air-scent dogs all work better at night because of scent, wind, and temperature considerations. Few night-time find statistics are currently available, but over 25% of lost Alzheimer's disease subjects have been located at night.[5] Finally, trackers, because they are often well directed and looking carefully at an area, can use a flashlight to provide all the needed illumination. In fact, it may also be easier to track at night since the light may be easily manipulated into any required angle.

3) *"The searchers are not properly trained nor prepared to search at night."*

This comment may be true of untrained volunteers. Even some "trained search teams" are reluctant to be deployed at night because they never train in this environment. However, this is the exception and not the rule. Almost all serious SAR training programs include night operations and navigation. The fear of deploying resources may be a result of ill-trained base staff not knowing how to run night operations and then citing one of the three excuses above to excuse their inexperience.

"A tracking stick is required."

A tracking stick is one of the tools new students use early in their career. In some areas it is also known as a signcutting, pace, stride, or step stick. The authors choose the term tracking stick because it is the most common term found in publications for a general SAR audience.[6] The tracker marks on the stick the subject's stride (distance from heel to heel) and the track measurements. The additional marks on the stick may include sole width, heel width, print length, or differences between left/right stride. The tracking stick, if wielded correctly, assists the tracker in finding and interpreting the next track or sign.

Unfortunately, many trackers become more interested in the tool than its function. They forget the stick is simply a set of training wheels meant to be used less frequently, and in some cases discarded, as their tracking skills mature. Some trackers have attached a mystical reverence to the tracking stick. Management often quietly smirks when they see any resource more interested in tools than the quality of the work product. Even worse, some inexperienced trackers punch holes into the tracks when using their sticks as a chin rest.

Other tracks have been destroyed when the student attempts to mark a track with circles or arcs. In their zeal, they neglect to see the true sign or next track. Therefore, some tracking instructors advocate carefully placing small Popsicle™ sticks slightly behind the heel print or sign. This helps avoid the tracking stick from becoming a track eraser.

Many students place O-rings or rubber bands on the stick to mark their measurements. In some cases they failed to measure and record the actual track measurements. Since Murphy sneaks along with every tracking team, especially out in the woods, the markers often move.

A locking tape measure with a stiff blade (around 12' in length and 0.5" in width) functions as an excellent alternative to the tracking stick. With the blade locked at the correct length it functions as a tracking stick. The tape measure is also highly versatile and light. The tracker can clip it to a belt, place it in a pocket, get the precise measurements to record, and avoid erasing tracks. After some practice, trackers can start to utilize their eyes to visually measure the stride length.

In some cases trackers need a hiking stick. Safety issues of navigating down a steep decline, crossing a stream, or moving up a treacherous slope, sometimes requires additional support. In these cases a thin tracking stick will not be adequate for the task. When fighting through heavy foliage many trackers are tempted to whack at the brush with a big hiking stick. Unfortunately, this may destroy subtle sign. All searchers should try to avoid hiking sticks when investigation indicates the lost subject uses a hiking stick.

"Tracking doesn't work in the woods or over difficult terrain."

Some trackers are known only as *track trap* people. Some tracking schools train only with track traps. This is, in itself, fine but track traps are not the only way one can track. Worsham has a tracking book dedicated largely to how to track on various ground cover— leaves, pine needles, grass, moss, gravel, frost, underbrush, and railroad tracks.[7]

1. *See appendix B for a list of suggested tracking courses.*
2. Robbins, R. (1977) " Mantracking" *Search and Rescue Magazine*
3. Bodziak (2000) *Footwear Impression Evidence, Second Edition.* CRC Press. Boca Raton,   FL.
4. Cassidy, Michael J. (1995) *Footwear Identification* Lightning Powder Co. Inc. Ottawa, ON.
5. Koester, R. (2000) *unpublished Alzheimer's disease data.* Charlottesville, VA.
6. LaValla, R., Stoffel, S., Jones, T. (1997) *Search Is An Emergency: A text for managing search operations* (4th Ed). Emergency Response Institute. Olympia, WA.
7. Worsham, C.E. (1992) *Techniques of Tracking on Various Ground Covers.* Madison Heights, VA.

7. Dog-Handling Misconceptions

When dealing with search resources that have not worked much with dog teams, misconceptions about what the dogs can or cannot do are frequently encountered. The following is not intended to be an all inclusive list, but it does cover some of the more frequently encountered situations reported in our area and attempts to explain the dog's capabilities in each situation. In some cases it is simply a matter of training, i.e., whether or not the handlers have trained and tested their dogs on such tasks. In all cases, when there is a question about what a dog can or cannot do, the handlers of the dogs available as search resources should be consulted.

"Dogs are useless unless a good scent article can be provided."

While some air-scent dogs are trained to be scent-discriminating, most are not. Most air-scent dogs are trained to locate the source of any human scent. Even those air-scent dogs that have been trained to scent discriminate can almost always work without a scent article. Since they try to locate the source of any human scent, air-scent dogs may find hikers, campers, or other searchers while in the field, but they may also locate the subject or articles left behind by the subject.

Bloodhounds, in many areas of the country, are the breed of dogs most frequently trained as scent-discriminating trailing dogs. However, just about any breed of dog can be trained in that manner. The training is much more important than the breed of dog.

There are a number of situations in which a bloodhound, or scent-discriminating trailing dog, can be of use when no scent articles are available. A few such situations will be discussed here, but the best advice, again, is to consult the handler whenever questions arise.

In some cases handlers can improvise scent articles. If, for example, the subject's car has been located and has not been contaminated by others, some handlers can improvise a scent article by laying sterile gauze on the car's seat for a short time.

If all available scent articles have been contaminated by others, but those people are still at the search site, the dog may be able to eliminate those individuals from consideration. Some handlers train their dogs to start from scent articles that have been handled by several people, then to check the individuals at the start of the trail and look for the trail of the individual that is not there. If park rangers found a missing person's campsite and checked the tent and other belongings left behind for identification, drugs, etc., those articles found in the campsite could still be used by some dog teams as scent articles. As long as the rangers that contaminated the campsite were available for the dog to check.

Many scent-discriminating dogs can be started from a known track. If tracking personnel discover a track that has a high probability of belonging to the subject, *and* they avoid any scent contamination of a section of that track, then many dogs could be started from that track.

Many police and sheriff's offices have patrol dogs that have been trained as *hot track* dogs. These dogs are frequently trained to follow the freshest (hottest) track in an area that has several tracks through it. Like the scent-discriminating dogs, they could be started from a track suspected of being the subject's that has not been contaminated by anyone else.

"Don't you need to keep your dog out of exhaust fumes/cigarette smoke/perfumes?"

This was the general opinion throughout the dog community for some time, and many handlers still believe this. However, recent experiences have shown that the problems are not nearly as severe as once thought. Dogs have successfully searched manufacturing areas, dump areas, airports, chemical plants, and still smoldering buildings, where there were seemingly overwhelming chemical or hydrocarbon odors. They have also successfully conducted water searches where heavy exhaust fumes from marine engines were unavoidable. Effectiveness and the dogs' ability to distinguish weak human scent are no doubt affected by such environments, but not to the point of negating the dog team's usefulness.

"Scent-discriminating dogs are useless if you cannot identify a valid PLS/LKP for the dog to pick up the trail."

Part of starting any scent-discriminating dog off on a track is allowing the dog to *cast about* for the location of the track after being exposed to the scent article. Many handlers carry this a step further and teach their dogs to cast over large areas for a track belonging to the subject. A dog with such training can be utilized to confirm or establish negative search results. For example, if it was known that a missing hiker's intermediate destination where Camp A, the dog could be used to cast for track around Camp A to determine whether or not the subject arrived at that point.

"Other resources should be held out of the field until search dogs have had a chance to search the area."

This may be a valid concern if a nearby local law enforcement agency has a dog that has been trained to run hot tracks and if that resource is readily available. Putting other searchers in the area would probably eliminate the hot track dog's utility. Decisions of this nature must be made by giving due consideration to the global search picture, i.e., the dog team's arrival time; search urgency; and availability of other resources including scent-discriminating trailing dogs and air-scent dogs. Even in instances in which the decision is made not to contaminate the PLS/LKP and adjacent areas, there should be other tasks that could be assigned to any waiting resources (containment and hasty tasks along trails and roads that are known to have had other traffic along them since the disappearance of the subject).

While all air-scent search dog handlers would love to have a pristine area to work because it improves the chances that their dogs will pick up faint scent left behind by the subject, such tactics are hardly ever justified. When wind and terrain conditions result in the scent from one search team being carried across nearby sectors, the utility of the air-scent dog team can be significantly reduced. Thus, in some cases, it may be necessary to stagger the start of tasks in nearby sectors to avoid strong distracting scent sources.

Keeping resources out of the field is a minor concern for the scent-discriminating trailing dogs. However, if the probability of obtaining a good scent article is low, but the confidence in the PLS or LKP is high, there could be an argument made for limiting access within some radius of the PLS/LKP to a very limited number of qualified tracking personnel. The tracking personnel would be searching for a valid track from which to start the scent-discriminating trailing dog. They would have to be aware of the need to avoid contamination of any located tracks.

"Air-scent dogs are not useful in urban areas."

In many cases air-scent dogs can be of use in urban areas. Parks, undeveloped woodland, and drainage ditches can all be searched by air-scent dog teams. In addition, many air-scent dog units now train their dogs to do building search. Such teams can be used to search for subjects that might be hiding to avoid location by visual search teams in such places as private homes, nursing homes, warehouses, or schools, as well as abandoned or empty buildings.

"Dogs never miss."

If the dog handler believes this, management has a *problem*. If the search manager believes this, the lost subject has a problem. If a dog team ever reports a POD higher than 75% and the area is not a paved parking lot, it's likely that they have over-reported their POD.

While a discussion of scent transport is well beyond the scope of this publication, it should be noted that a myriad of conditions contribute to the success or failure of each individual search task. Wind direction, spotty scent pools, contaminating scent sources, and handler fatigue can all contribute to missed detection/find by even a focused, well-trained dog. Dog teams are another "tool" for searching -- they are not infallible. Many search coordinators can relate stories of ground teams finding a subject in an area "cleared" by a search dog team. In some cases a *not completely trained dog* actually found the subject but did not indicate this to the handler. Dogs are a great contributor, and they can cover large areas effectively, but there's never 100% POD with *any* one resource. In the long run, overstating a resource's capability only decreases the value of that resource in the eyes of management. In some areas of the country overstating has resulted in resources no longer being requested.

8. Expected Man-Tracking Skills

The tracker should be able to signcut and track effectively and efficiently, day or night, on various ground covers, soil, and weather conditions at a high rate of speed.

The tracker should be trained on leaves, pine needles, above-ground vegetation, grass, aged humus, and various soils. A tracker working with dog resources must be able to adapt to different speeds because a handler may go from a slow walk to a run.

Be prepared for anything! There are many dangers out there that can crop up when least expected.

Both trackers and handlers need to be prepared to work in base by assisting with investigation, writing tasks, or interacting with the **legal responsible agent**.

All searches have the potential of turning into a criminal investigation. All searchers must be properly trained to function safely in the full range of environmental conditions found in their region. Teams have found themselves faced with hazardous materials, confined space environments, and bullets whizzing overhead.

All trackers need to be trained in and practice not only their tracking skills but also SAR skills.

In order to function safely in the environment the tracker requires training in medical skills, radio operations, land navigation, proper personal equipment, and basic survival skills.

Be prepared to operate as a team leader. The appointed team leader is ultimately in charge of the team. Search managers should have a clear set of expectations for and from the team. Usually the handler is the leader, however.

In many areas of the country the dog handler will be appointed the team leader. When trackers are coupled with dog handlers the task may be primarily a dog task or a tracking task. Depending on the purpose of the task the incident staff may choose the appropriate person to be the team leader. The designation of team leader may also be based on the training skills of each participant. In some SAR systems dog handlers may not be skilled in land navigation or radio communications and the tracker may be utilized as the team leader. On some tracking only teams, the leader may use the term team coordinator. While out on the task, the team coordinator may change multiple times.

The tracker may be asked to do anything.

In the world of SAR, expect the unexpected. This may include helping to lift a dog over a fence. Tasks may also require crawling in storm drains, scrambling up 45 degree drainages, passing through dense, seemingly impassable underbrush, or providing medical care and initial stabilization to the subject.

Be prepared to perform long tasks in any type of terrain and in any weather condition, even at night.

Night operations are often required due to urgency, the nature of the search, or to increase the efficiency of the search. Scenting conditions may be better at night and therefore increase the effectiveness of canine teams. Incident management may attempt to draw up tasks that only last 4-6 hours. However, they are unable to predict all factors so a team may spend 8-12 hours in the field. All personnel must go out into the field prepared for unexpected delays.

Be in good physical shape.

Canine teams may move at a high rate of speed and perform long tasks. Some trailing and tracking handlers often work at a virtual run. Most air-scent dog handlers work at a moderate walk. Good conditioning is also essential to help prevent heat and cold disorders. Any searcher who is concentrating on his next breath cannot effectively signcut, track, or handle a search dog.

Carry outdoor and survival gear, tracking kit, different size light sources, and provisions that coincide with the task and weather conditions.

The appropriate equipment for the task should be carried, factoring in worst-case scenarios for weather and other changes. See Appendix A for a list of supplies that should be included in a tracking kit.

Maintain a detailed log of all tasks and training.

A log is critical if the tracker is called on to provide testimony in court. Maintaining a log will assist the tracker in learning from tasks and training. A log may include, but not be limited to, times called out, time arrived at base, beginning and ending of all tasks, search area, names of team members, name of responsible agent and point of contact, observations and problems on all tasks, and weather information starting from two weeks or more prior to the person's disappearance. If available, information on suspected footwear, description sketches of possible tracks, measurements, and any tracking observations should be recorded. If a clue or track is located that may qualify as criminal evidence, the location must be logged and a chain of custody must be maintained.

Understand the signcutting and tracking problems created and the lower probability of detection (POD) of clues, sign, and tracks due to operating at a higher rate of speed.

The tracker may lose focus and the ability to make a careful check of areas of interest when working with a rapidly moving dog team. The tracker should mark on the map areas of interest for future tracking tasks.

Be prepared to operate radio communications.

Handling communications will create obstacles for the tracker, such as losing baselines. Know the communications protocol for the area, including frequency, channels, and team identifier. Consider requesting a walker to handle communications. However, incident staff may not be able to assign a third person due to lack of resources or because some dogs become distracted by larger teams.

Be prepared to handle land navigation.

Trackers who agree to navigate must know how to navigate accurately, quickly, and on the run. Marking the map with wind directions and hits may also be necessary. Handling land navigation will create obstacles to tracking. Consider requesting a walker to handle land navigation. Once again, management may refuse this requests for the reasons stated above. When working with tracking/trailing dogs the handler's entire focus may be on working the dog. If working with an air-scent dog, the handler will often attempt to navigate at the same time. However, during **strong alerts** the dog may rapidly follow the scent and the handler will be in hot pursuit. Not only will the alert location need to be accurately plotted but the tracker will become responsible for all aspects of land navigation. In addition, at the conclusion of the task or in response to an urgent clue the team may be reassigned to another task area. Once again, the tracker may be responsible for this rapid and critical navigation.

Trackers may be asked to help carry additional water for the dog.

Dogs require a lot of water, especially in dry or hot areas. It is difficult for the handler to carry sufficient water for both the handler and the dog. Because they lack the ability to sweat, dogs must consume a lot of water to aid in the cooling process. If the nasal passages become dry, this significantly reduces the dog's ability to detect scent. Heat disorders may quickly affect dogs that become dehydrated. A tracker may be requested to carry an extra gallon. This may make bending over sign and tracks more difficult.

Do not contaminate scent articles or footprints.

The scent-discriminating dog handler will be suspicious of an article of unknown or questionable origin. The tracker should allow the handler to retrieve and handle any scent articles unless he has been trained and/or requested to obtain the article.

The team should initially avoid touching or contaminating the article. If a good chance exists that the item belong to the search subject, base should be contacted. The team should be asked to preserve the clue in order to maintain the chain of evidence and for potential follow up by a scent-discriminating dog team.

Upon finding a footprint that the tracker feels may be related to the search subject, the team should take steps to minimize contamination of the area and preserve the track. The tracker may contact base and inquire about the availability of a scent-discriminating dog. The team may be requested to stay with the tracks until the scent-discriminating dog team arrives or to follow the tracks.

9. Expected Dog-Handling Skills

The canine team should be in adequate physical condition for the assigned task.

If the tracking person has concerns about the canine handler's physical condition and feels this might compromise team safety, the tracking person may bring these concerns to the base personnel.

The dog should be well socialized to people and other dogs.

Aggression toward the general public, the lost person, other dogs, and searchers is not acceptable in SAR. All dog units should have standards that tests the dog's aggression and behavior. However, do not always expect dogs to be friendly.

The dog should be transportable.

Dogs may need to be transported in confined conditions with or without the handler. The dog should not display undue stress or aggression towards the handler, other people, or other dogs. At times, the dog may need to be transported on the handler's lap.

The canine team/team leader should be willing to listen to other team members.

The team leader should allow team members to help formulate a plan that will enhance the task, the tracker's skills and the skills of other team members. Always keep in mind that some canine teams cannot change the way their dog works just for other's benefit. Many times it will be possible to formulate a task plan that will enhance the opportunities to use tracking skills. If the canine team understands signcutting and tracking and how this discipline can fit into the task at hand, they should discuss their thoughts and ideas on how to proceed.

The handler should have the appropriate equipment for the assigned task, terrain, weather, and length of task.

As with all search team members, the handler should be prepared for unexpected changes in weather, terrain, and changes in task duration. It is not uncommon to reassign dog and tracking tasks in the field in order to respond to new clues. Therefore, the dog handlers must carry additional food and water for the dog. During the summer, a larger dog may require a gallon or more for a four-hour task.

The canine team should not leave other team members.

Many canine teams are not used to working with "outsiders." Some dog units may not have much experience working on searches where resources from different organizations are integrated onto the same team. This may be a result of "the way it is always done," from an operational philosophy, or due to unfamiliarity with other resources. Do not take this personally. In such situations it is absolutely necessary that both the handler and tracker have a common understanding of the task's objectives, team leader, and agree upon the tactics they will employ; prior to starting the task. There are times a handler may ask the tracker to hold a position while working out a hot alert. In these cases, the purpose of holding position is to maintain the point in the search pattern where the team broke off. If the alert turns out negative the handler will return to this point. In all cases, the tracking person should plot the point on the map. However, this possibility of separation should have been planned for by ensuring communication within the team. This may include extra radios or cyalume sticks at night. It is the responsibility of the team leader/handler to eventually find team members to ensure team safety.

Dog handlers should be at least adequate at land navigation.

In many areas handlers have years of land navigation experience. Dog unit organizations usually test the navigation skills of the handlers. In some areas handlers do not learn and practice land navigation. Instead they are taught to rely on a team member or the team leader to perform navigation. In these areas, when the search management decides to pair trackers and handlers, they must make certain that the assigned tracker has sufficient navigation skills. Likewise, every team member should ensure that the search team to which they are assigned is properly trained and equipped. To enhance search effectiveness each team member capable of land navigation should have a map and use it to plot the team's progress.

If in the handler's opinion the dog is not "working," the handler should be willing to alter his task and/or search strategy.

If a relevant clue, sign, or track has been found by the handler or another member of the canine team the tracker may follow up within the task area. Other times the handler may decide to abort the task and return to base. On those tasks that require the team to walk an extensive distance to reach the task area, the tracking person should be given the opportunity to look for sign.

As a SAR specialist, the dog handler should train on a regular basis.

It takes a considerable amount of time and effort to prepare a dog for search and rescue work. It is not a "do and forget" activity. The dogs must be trained regularly to maintain their proficiency and periodically retested to validate the skills. Unit records should include past training schedules, topics of training points, and personnel attendance records. Many handlers find maintaining a mission/training log helpful, especially if involved in criminal cases.

The canine team should have been tested against team or regional standards.

All SAR units fielding canine teams for search operations should have a set of written standards that define their testing procedures and methodology and the skills that both the dog and handler must demonstrate in order to be certified. These standards should be made available to any legally responsible agent or other SAR units.

The lack of a written standard does not imply that the dog team is incompetent. Many handlers with years of experience have made dozens of finds without a piece of paper in pretty fonts stating their certification. This may particularly be true with law enforcement resources. However, without standards search management must place the dog team's reliability at the lowest level. Fortunately, if the team proves itself on previous searches and favorable word of mouth spreads, then management can learn to trust the team. Clearly, this represents a less than ideal method of evaluating resources. On the other hand, testing and certification only represents the skill set the handler possessed at a single point in time. The skill of the dog team will either grow or degrade over time depending upon training and search experience.

At the very least the testing should be comprised of a day- time and nighttime problem typical of the task assignments in the local areas. Units may include additional tests for such specialties as article search, cadaver search, water search, or disaster search scenarios. In addition, some units require dog handlers to maintain varying levels of proficiency in search management.

Currently, no general consensus exists on what a practical test must contain. Different regional environments and operational considerations significantly influence the types of skills needed by both the dog and handler. In some areas, SAR units feel that their dog teams must not only be trained in air-scent search but also in scent-discriminating trailing. In other areas disaster search may be of primary importance.

Handlers in some areas are expected to be functional search managers because of a scarcity or unwillingness to use other specialized resources. In other areas, dog handlers may be viewed as just one of the assets that can be assigned to a team leader that is responsible for the navigation, the tactics, and techniques used by the team.

No matter what the operational philosophy is within a region, a SAR dog unit's standard should define the minimum set of skills that each dog and handler must have to function effectively in that environment. However, many units will go far beyond that in their training and testing programs.

The canine team/leader should act and treat team members in a professional manner at all times.

10. Tracker's Concerns About Canines

Most trackers have not worked with a handler.

Working together is still a new concept in many areas. Resource reputations may have been previously damaged by arrogance or overstated skills. Trackers new to this tactic will find it difficult to operate at the dog team's increased speed.

Trackers may be skeptical about the abilities of dogs.

For many people it is difficult to understand how the dog's senses are so much better than a human's. Because it is impossible to independently verify the dog's performance in search situations, the tracker may doubt the dog's abilities. Learning how the dog and handler train or practicing with the canine team may help overcome these doubts.

Trackers may be afraid of dogs.

Many people, due to bad experiences with untrained animals, may have a fear of dogs. Search and Rescue dogs typically have written training standards that require the dogs to be well socialized and obedient. Air-scent dogs undergo practical obedience and socialization testing. Trailing dogs such as bloodhounds have less rigid socialization requirements. Trackers should take some time to familiarize themselves with the dog before starting the task. No tracker should ever "feed" their hand to any dog without the handler's permission. Trackers should also avoid contact with the dog when it is still in the handler's vehicle or the crate.

Trackers may feel the canine handler does not appreciate or understand their specialized skills.

Unfortunately, in most circumstances the handler will not be familiar with the skills of the tracker. Without a complete understanding of the tactics and speed at which a tracker normally operates, the dog handler cannot appreciate the extra stress the tracker experiences when working with a dog team. The tracker must also understand that under some circumstances base management did not really intend for the tracker to spend a lot of time tracking. Instead, they simply wanted the tracker to augment the dog team and fill in some holes. The tracker must communicate to the dog handler a basic overview of what the he hopes to accomplish. While this overview should be done before the task begins, in a more ideal world, the tracker and handler would have trained together.

Utilizing canine teams with a tracker is a new concept in many areas.

Trackers may be leery of how the team will work if they have never worked with another canine team. The trackers may not understand why management sent them with a dog team that does not really allow trackers to track. Many trackers are accustomed to having total control of the team and are challenged by a possible secondary role. Without prior training some problems are almost guaranteed to arise during the task. Few locations around the country use trackers and dog handlers together. The reasons may include management's lack of understanding of how the resources work, the view that both are separate SAR specialists who cannot work together, lack of sufficient resources to combine, personality conflicts, or perhaps simply that nobody ever thought of combining the two resources.

11. Handler's Concerns About Trackers

Most canine handlers have not worked with a tracker.

They may be skeptical of tracking or especially utilizing tracking with canine teams. Working together is still a new concept in many areas. Like the tracker, handlers train for and respond to searches so they can perform their speciality. Unlike the tracker, the handler lacks the flexibility to change tactics due to the dog's training. Throughout handlers' training, they are taught to adjust their behavior to maximize the dog's effectiveness. When teamed with someone that appears to want to do the opposite, conflict arises. Resource reputations may have been previously damaged by arrogance or overstated skills. Both types of resources will need to learn to make applicable adjustments.

The handler may be skeptical of the tracker's reported skill level and experience.

In many areas the "I-be-a-tracker" person, who has had a one- hour tracking course, is still causing problems with his claims that he is "the tracker, the solution and salvation for all of the search's problems." For this reason it is important for trackers to communicate their level of training, recertification, continuing education, and practice time in the field.

The handlers may be concerned about the inherent dangers of working with personnel untrained in canine teamwork, law enforcement, or related tactics.

This may be more of a problem in regions where the various types of SAR teams are not used to working together. In order to increase comfort with mixed teams (combined resources from different groups or organizations) groups should train or hold simulations together. It is important that tracking personnel are trained in a broad set of SAR skills including navigation, communications, first-aid, overview of different resource tactics, site management, and evidence preservation. The handler may also be concerned with how the tracker may react in an emergency or life-threatening situation.

The handler will be concerned about the canine team's safety and may prefer not to be burdened with any inexperienced person.

It is important for the tracking person to communicate their field experience to the handler.

Utilizing a tracking person with a canine team is a new concept in many areas.

The handler may be leery of how the team will work if they have never worked with a tracking person before. Previous experience with tracking personnel may have been negative. Many canine teams are accustomed to total control of the team; in most cases the canine handler will be the team leader.

Law enforcement personnel are often leery of trusting civilians for many of the reasons listed above.

12. Training Suggestions

Throughout this book it has emphasized the need for trackers and dog handlers to train together. However, the text has neglected, until now, to provide instruction on how they might effectively train together. This material was learned over hundreds of practice sessions and actual searches. It is our hope all searchers can both learn from the author's mistakes and also find new methods to allow these two important resources to work together as a team.

In order to successfully train as a team, different techniques are required with air-scent, tracking, and trailing dogs. One important aspect of this book was providing information on how each of these dogs and trackers work. It is important to realize that because each type of dog works differently, each practice session (and clearly each search) must be set up differently for both the handler and tracker.

Reading books, attending lectures, and other forms of academic learning make an excellent first step. However, both tracking and dog handling are similar, because nothing is truly learned without field practice. The handler must learn the nuances of how the dog works and communicates through body language. For the tracker, seeing is everything. For the dog handler, the best method of understanding tracking is to attend some awareness courses. Several tracking courses are listed in the appendix. Next, practice with a knowledgeable (and mellow) tracker or tracking group. The tracker's best approach is to become an associate member of a dog group. At times this might mean hiding from air-scent dogs or setting down trails for tracking and trailing dogs. This is an important part of the learning process. In all cases, trackers and handlers will forge the personal relationships that make them better able to overcome the stress of the search environment.

Several different exercises are suggested to start the training process. They are specifically designed for each different type of dog. They provide a good start. However, as the handler and tracker get more experience working with each other they will quickly exhaust this limited list. Soon they will develop new training exercises. It is impossible to train for all the bizarre circumstances that occur on searches. However, it can be fun to make the attempt.

Exercise 1. The tracker observes a typical dog task.

An experienced air-scent dog handler should be assigned a typical task with a tracker as the *walker*. Both resources should briefly state their capabilities (see Chapter 5 on tracker-handler communication). The tracker should learn from the handler how they will be positioned during the task. The handler will serve as the lead on this exercise and work the dog in the normal fashion. Whenever possible, the handler should explain what they are doing and key features of the task. As the terrain allows, different tactics should be used on the task. Ideally, a subject should be placed in the sector to allow the tracker to observe an alert and find. Trackers should try to serve as the walker with several different dog teams and types.

Exercise 2. The handler observes a tracking task.

An experienced tracker should set up a tracking task with a dog handler (no dog) as the *walker*. The tracker will serve as the lead on this exercise. Whenever possible, the tracker should explain what she is doing and why. A PLS should be set up by either the tracker, or preferably another tracker, so that the tracks can be *easily* located. The tracks should leave the PLS following a predetermined direction of travel. The tracker should follow these tracks while giving the dog handler explanations as to the usage of their tracking tactics, aging, etc.

This task should have at least several turn offs, should go through several different ground covers, utilize several different tactics, and end up finishing with a find. This exercise can be repeated in more difficult environments, can be extended in distance, and can even have the dog handler *practice* signcutting and tracking.

Air-scent Dogs

Handler decides where good track traps are located.

The tracker gives the handler a brief demonstration on track traps. The tracker should mention how a track trap can be both the more classic large area of soft sand/dirt or even a small quarter-sized area of dirt that allows easy detection of a partial sole pattern. A subject does not *have* to be in the area for this exercise. The dog handler is assigned a sector that contains several different types of potential track traps. The handler takes the lead and works the sector. While working the sector the handler should stop at what he believes are good track traps. The tracker should provide positive feedback as appropriate.

The tracker detects the dog's alert.

An assistant will need to serve as a subject and hide within the assigned search area. Before the task begins the handler must brief the tracker on how his dog alerts. The handler proceeds with the task. The goal of this exercise is for the tracker to recognize the air-scent dog's alert. This exercise can easily be combined with other exercises. With some air-scent dogs it may be possible to observe different alerts for alive human, cadaver, and article finds. The tracker should always be scanning the environment (which includes the dog!).

Start at PLS, tracker starts and switches lead to handler.

A PLS should be established and tracks laid down. The difficulty of the trail should be varied depending on the experience of the tracker. The tracker should be allowed to start working at the PLS. The handler should have the dog off-lead. This will allow the handler to determine if the dog has the habit of going over to the tracker and accidentally stepping on the track. The dog may also start walking over other potential tracks. The handler and dog can work on techniques to keep the dog under control. The tracker can give suggestions on how best to position the dog when they are working a track. After the tracker gets a direction of travel the handler should take the lead and start working the area. The tracker can work on detecting any additional sign. The handler may also work on finding additional track traps.

Tracker and handler switch leads during the task.

The handler should start as the lead for this exercise. The handler should identify a natural point to switch the lead to the tracker. This might be because he finds a track trap, the dog needs to rest, or the dog does not appear to be working. The tracker might then use tactics such as zig-zag, feature, or perimeter depending on terrain, nature of assigned area, etc. In thicker terrain or foliage, if no passage is found, the tracker might put more emphasis on looking for track traps. The task might be set up so it crosses several excellent track traps or features (stream, dirt, road, fence-lines). The handler should ideally give the tracker the opportunity to work these features. If possible set actual tracks in one of these features. However, the purpose of this exercise is not for the tracker to follow the trail (if found) track-by-track, but simply to locate the track. The tracker should then switch the lead back to the dog handler. Consider placing a subject near the end of the task for the dog to locate.

Another twist on this exercise is to let the handler take the lead during the first pass of the assigned area. On the second pass (or return trip) the tracker takes the lead. No subject is placed in the area during the first pass. During the second pass a subject may be placed in the area. This will allow the handler some feedback on how well his dog may work when he does not have the lead and is *following* the tracker.

Tracking/Trailing Dogs

While both tracking and trailing dogs work differently, the types of exercises for the tracker and dog handler are similar. The major difference between working with tracking/trailing and air-scent dogs is the faster pace and greater reluctance of stopping the tracking/ trailing dogs. However, with all three dogs the initial exercises are the same. The tracker should repeat exercise one, observing a typical dog task, with each type of dog. The tracker should also be willing to show each of the three types of handlers a tracking task (as specified in Exercise 2.)

Handler finds track traps, without dog.

The tracker gives the handler a brief demonstration and explanation on track traps. A subject does not have to be in the area for this exercise. The dog handler should leave the dog back at base. The dog handler is assigned a trail that has several different types of potential track traps. The handler takes the lead and works the trail. While working the trail the handler should stop at what he believes are good track traps. The tracker should provide positive feedback as appropriate.

Handler finds tracks in the track traps.

Tracks are established along a trail that includes several different types of track traps. The handler should leave her dog back at the training base. The handler is given the task of attempting to locate sign along the trail. The tracker should vary the pace from working slowly to the speed the handler normally works with her dog. The tracker should demonstrate different methods to increase detection in track traps.

Start at PLS.

A PLS should be established and tracks laid down. The difficulty of the trail should be varied depending on the experience of the tracker. The handler should have the dog in its working harness. The tracker should be allowed to start working at the PLS when working with a trailing dog. When working with a tracking dog, the tracker may be required to stay away from the PLS to avoid contamination. After the tracker gets a direction of travel the handler should take the lead and start working the area. The tracker should avoid informing the handler of the direction of travel. The trailing dog handler will probably want to start at the PLS. After the dog team starts going in the same direction the tracker may provide confirmation of the trail. The tracker may point out the impact the dog and handler have on any tracks that were located and marked.

Practice tracking on the fly solo.

One of the greatest challenges facing a tracker is *tracking on the fly*. Trackers commonly crawl on the ground, look at a track from several angles, index the ground, and perform several other time-consuming steps with each track. Once the tracking/trailing dog is hot on the trail the handler is often being pulled along by the dog. This leaves little to no time for the tracker to detect sign. Therefore, more experienced trackers should practice finding sign while moving at a faster pace. Since this requires practice, the tracker should first start without a dog handler present. Tracks should be laid. The tracker should then practice detecting the sign without stopping and at a normal walking pace. After several attempts a second walker may be added. The purpose of the second walker is simply to set the pace. This forces the tracker to keep moving. As the tracker gains experience the pace of the walker should be increased. The tracker at times may have to get down into the dirt to verify a track. The next couple of moments may then be spent sprinting to catch back up to the pace walker.

Practice tracking on the fly with dog.

After the tracker has gained some experience tracking on the fly solo, they may graduate to practicing the skill with the canine team. Once again, tracks are laid in terrain that has several track traps to start. The canine handler works the trail in the normal fashion. When working with trailing dogs it is important to realize that the scent may be blown several feet or even yards away from the trail. Therefore, the dog and handler may be fighting through heavy brush 10 feet away from the actual trail. In this situation, the tracker may have the opportunity to work a trail while the handler suffers in the brush. Trackers need to be careful to not always follow exactly in the same path of the trailing dog. When initially practicing these techniques, shorter tasks are required. When practicing with the canine team, it is important for the tracker to realize the canine team, under normal circumstances, does not like to stop once the dog is on the trail. After considerable experience the handler may choose to see the results of stopping the dog.

Trackers Working With Canine Teams
Checklist

☑ Be able to signcut and track on the run.
☑ Be prepared for anything.
☑ Be prepared to operate as the team leader.
☑ Be prepared to perform long tasks.
☑ Be in good physical shape.
☑ Carry an outdoor and tracking kit.
☑ Maintain a log.
☑ Know the problem of moving at a high rate of speed.
☑ Be prepared to handle radio communications.
☑ Be prepared to handle land navigation.
☑ Be prepared to carry extra water.
☑ Do not contaminate scent articles or clues.
☑ Ask the handler what is expected.
☑ Advise the handler about your capabilities.
☑ Explain what you may be doing and why.
☑ Communicate tracking procedures with the handler.
☑ Inquire if anyone has had any tracking training.
☑ Explain track traps.
☑ Request breaks near track traps.
☑ Inform canine team of medical problems.
☑ Do not touch or talk to the dog without permission.
☑ Do not exceed training and expertise.
☑ Keep the task safe.
☑ Inform the handler of anything found.
☑ Stay where directed by the canine team.
☑ Do not talk unnecessarily on task.
☑ Do not ask unnecessary questions during the task.
☑ Do not shoot from the hip.
☑ Is the canine team prepared for the task?
☑ Is the dog socialized?
☑ Is the canine team listening to the tracker's comments?

Appendix A.
Suggested Tracking Items[1]

These items are not required but are suggested equipment. Equivalent gear and an improvised tracking kit (tools) would be acceptable. This list may be modified to adapt to seasonal and special conditions. Not all of this equipment would be carried into the field but should be available to the individual on the mission in some form. This may include a vehicle cache or pack left at base.

Tracking-Specific Items

☑ Tracking stick or measuring tape
☑ Measuring tape (6'-12')
☑ Calipers and dividers
☑ Popsicle™ sticks - about three dozen with reflective tape
☑ Kite string - at least fifty feet
☑ Handheld mirror or signal mirror
☑ Magnifying glass-5X-stronger may distort
☑ Waterproof notebook/pad with pens or pencils
☑ Tweezers
☑ Light Source - large and small with color lenses and extra batteries. A headlamp should be carried for use in difficult terrain and/or in evacuations.
☑ Laser pointer
☑ Camera and film - may use digital or instamatic
☑ Casting materials - dental stone recommended

General SAR Gear

☑ Orienteering type compass - A GPS may also be carried but you must be proficient with map and compass
☑ Flagging tape
☑ Flash cards for reference

☑ Wind shell jacket with hood

☑ Water resistant jacket or parka with hood

☑ Rain pants or chaps (gaiters)

☑ Heavy wool shirts, pants, and sweaters as required

☑ Long underwear made of wool, silk, polypropylene or other suitable synthetic material

☑ Wool stocking cap or balaclava. Scarf is recommended with stocking cap.

☑ Heavy wool socks with lightweight liner socks

☑ Leather gloves with wool liners. Mittens are suggested for extremely cold weather.

☑ Backpacking or mountaineering boots appropriate to the terrain and weather conditions

☑ Backpack or fanny pack suitable for day use

☑ Canteens or water bottles containing a minimum of 2 quarts of water

☑ Multi-blade pocket knife

☑ Whistle

☑ Waterproof matches or other fire starter

☑ Personal first-aid kit with your medications if applicable

☑ Storm shelter, tent, tube tent, space blanket, etc.

☑ Two-day minimum supply of quick energy food

☑ Two 30-gallon, heavy-duty leaf bags

☑ A sleeping bag and ensolite, or similar, sleeping pad

☑ Handheld radio operating on required frequencies.

Note: Fleece is the fabric of choice for cold weather clothing but an insulating material such as wool or other synthetics may be substituted if necessary.[2] Down and cotton are not acceptable.

1. Fuller, G. (2000) *Field Team Signcutter Workbook.* dbS Productions. Charlottesville, VA.

2. Hamlet, M. (2000) The Science of clothing for the Outdoors. *Wilderness Medicine.* 17:1:1

Appendix B.
Suggested Tracking Courses

Human Tracking Schools

The Tracking Institute
Greg Fuller
P. O. Box 197
Onancock, VA 23417
1-804-293-5502

The Southwest Association of Trackers
Owen Couch
P.O. Box 1648
Gallup, NM 87305
1-505-778-5311

Universal Tracking Services, Inc.
Joel C. Hardin
15200 S. W. Twin Fir Road
Lake Oswego, OR 97035
1-360-966-7707

Tactical Tracking Operations School, Inc.
David Scott-Donelan
P. O. Box 2523
Mesquite, NV 89024
1-520-347-5377

Nature and Vision Tracking School
Charles Worsham
446 Thomas Road
Madison Heights, Virginia 24572
1-804-846-1987

Albert (Ab) S. Taylor's Tracking School
Ab Taylor
1219 Arnold Way
Alpine, CA 91901
1-619-445-8032

Animal Tracking Schools

Nature and Vision Tracking School
Charles Worsham
446 Thomas Road
Madison Heights, VA 24572
1-804-846-1987

A Naturalist's World
Dr. James Halfpenny
P. O. Box 989, 206 5th St. West
Gardiner, MT 59030
1-406-848-9458

Programs in Tracking
Paul Rezendes
3833 Bearsden Road
Royalston, MA 01368-9400
1-978-249-8810

Appendix C.
Tracking Bibliography

This limited bibliography is meant to give beginning tracking students a list of basic books and manuals that they may find useful in their education and growth in animal and human tracking. Also, some material for this course comes from some of these publications. You will have to determine if the following have any value. Remember, you can only judge tracking material (written or oral) by dirt time and proving. Nothing replaces dirt time!

Arnheim, R. (1974) *Art and Visual Perception.* Univ. of Ca. Press, Los Angles, CA

Arnheim, R. (1969) *Visual Thinking.* Univ. of Ca. Press, Los Angles, CA

Bang, P., Dahlstrom, P. (1974) *Animal Tracks and Signs.* William Collins Sons and Co. Ltd. St. James Place, London

Bodziak, W. (2000) *Footwear Impression Evidence: Second Edition.* CRC Press, Boca Raton, FL

Brown, T. (1999) *The Science and Art of Tracking.* Berkley Publishing Group, NY, NY

Brown, T. (1983) *Tom Brown's Field Guide to Nature Observation and Tracking.* Berkley Publishing Group, NY, NY

Cassidy, M. (1995) *Footwear Identification.* Lightning Powder Co, Salem, OR.

Combat Tracker and Tracker Dog Training and Employment. Field Manual 7-42

De Mello, A. (1990) *Awareness.* Doubleday/Bantam, NY, NY

Edwards, B. (1989) *Drawing on the Right Side of the Brain.* Jeremy P. Tarcher Inc. Los Angeles, CA

Fineman, M. (1981) *The Nature of Visual Illusion.* Dover Publication, Mineola, NY

Forest, L. (1988) *Field Guide to Tracking Animals in Snow.* Stackpole Books, Harrisburg, PA

Fuller, G. (1999) *Guidelines for Non-Tracking Personnel Operating with Signcutting and Tracking Teams.* Privately printed. Onancock, VA

Fuller, G. (1998) *Guidelines for Tracking Personnel Operating with a Canine Team.* Onancock, VA

Fuller, G. (1998) *Guidelines for Tracking Trainees and Walkers.* Search and Rescue Tracking Institute, Onancock, VA

Gaulke, D. (1998) *The Revival of Traditional Animal Tracking.* Masters Thesis. Prescott College, Prescott, AZ

Gray, J. (1968) *Animal Locomotion* WW Norton & Company, NY, NY

Gregory, R. (1997) *Eye and Brain, The Psychology of Seeing.* Princeton University Press, Princeton, NJ

Halfpenny, J., Ozanne, R. (1989) *Winter; An Ecological Handbook.* Johnson Books, Boulder, CO

Halfpenny, J. (1986) *Field Guide to Mammal Tracking.* Johnson Books, Boulder.

Hanratty, T. (1997) *Tracking Man and Beast.* Medicine Hawk Publications, Inc., Milwaukee, WI

Hoffman, D. (1998) *Visual Intelligence.* W.W. Norton & Company, NY, NY

Hubel, D. (1995) *Eye, Brain, and Vision.* Scientific American Library, NY, NY

Inman, V., Ralston, H., Todd, F. (1981) *Human Walking.* Williams & Wilkins, Baltimore, MD

Kearney, J. (1978) *Tracking: A Blueprint for Learning How.* Pathways Press, El Cajon, CA

Krishnamurti, J. (1987) *The Awakening of Intelligence.* Harper Collins, San Francisco, CA

Liebenberg, L. (1990) *The Art of Tracking.* David Philip Publishers, Cape Town and Johannesburg, RSA

Murie, O. (1974) *Animal Tracks in Peterson Field Guide Series.* Houghton Mifflin Company, Boston, MA

Muybridge, E. (1957) *Animals in Motion.* Dover Publications, NY, NY

Muybridge, E. (1955) *The Human Figure in Motion.* Dover Pub., NY, NY

Rezendes, P. (1999) *Tracking & the Art of Seeing: Second Ed.* Harper Perennial Inc. NY, NY

Rezendes, P. (1998) *The Wild Within; Adventures in Nature and Animal Teachings.* Penguin Putnam Inc. Putnam, NY

Robbins, R. (1977) "Mantracking" *Search and Rescue Magazine*, Montrose,

Samuels, M., Samuels, N. (1975) *Seeing with the Mind's Eye.* Random House, NY, NY

Scott-Donelan, D. (1997) *Tactical Tracking Operations.* Paladin Press, Boulder, CO

Stearn, J. (1976) *The Power of Alpha-Thinking.* Signet, NY, NY

Surya-Das, Lama (1997) *Awakening the Buddha Within.* Broadway Books, NY, NY

Taylor, A., Cooper, D. (1990) *Fundamentals of Mantracking.* Emergency Response Institute, Inc. Olympia, WA

Virginia, Commonwealth of, Department of Emergency Services (1997) *Field Team Signcutter Standards.* http://www.vdes.state.va.us/emanager/sar/ftsstand.htm

Worsham, C. (1996) *Locating Tracks - Visual Perception and the File Cabinet.* Madison Heights, VA

Worsham, C. (1995) *Camouflage: The Art of Deception.* Madison Hts. VA

Worsham, C. (1992) *Techniques of Tracking on Various Ground Covers.* Madison Heights, VA

Glossary

Air-Scent Dog: A search dog that is trained to detect and indicate airborne human scent.

Alert: 1) A status indicating a likelihood of a SAR activation for a SAR resource. 2) observable changes in an air-scenting dog's focus, intensity, and body language that indicate it has detected human scent. 3) **weak alert**- the dog briefly shows heightened interest in following a scent, but does not follow it far or long. 4) **strong alert**- the dog may stay focused on working out the source of the scent for a number of minutes, and may lead the team hundreds of yards.

Agency Administrator: The official having legal responsibility for the emergency response to a SAR incident. This person is also known as the "Responsible Agent."

Bark indication: 1) Once a dog has located the subject the dog barks to notify the handler. 2) Once a dog has located the subject it returns to the handler and barks.

Baselines: Establishing the normal conditions found within the environment.

Bloodhounds: A breed of dog. The term is often incorrectly used to refer to a scent-discriminating trailing dog.

Bringsel: An object, often a strip of leather, that hangs from an air-scent dog's collar. Upon locating a subject the dog puts the bringsel in its mouth and returns to the handler.

Cast: The action of a scent-discriminating trailing dog of searching for a scent trail after exposure to a scent article.

Dog Team: One trained dog handler and one trained SAR dog. Under most circumstances it will also contain a team walker.

Find-Refind: The two steps in a chained sequence of behavior. After a dog makes a find, it gives the handler an indication that it made a find, and then leads the handler back to the subject (refind).

Handler: A tracking, trailing, or air-scent dog handler.

Incident: An occurrence or event, either human-caused or natural phenomena, that requires action by emergency service personnel to prevent or minimize loss of life or damage to property and/or natural resources.

Incident Command Post (ICP): The location at which the primary command functions are executed and usually co-located with the incident base.

Incident Commander (IC): The individual responsible for the overall on-scene management of all incident operations.

Indication: Trained behavior that a dog uses to demonstrate to the handler that he has found a person (or, perhaps, an article). Common indications include the bark alert, find-refind, and bringsel.

Initial Planning Point (IPP): Base point from which median distances are plotted. It may be the same as the Point Last Seen (PLS) or the Last Known Position (LKP).

Last **Known Position (LKP)**: The last known location for the missing subject as determined by verifiable physical evidence such as a discarded object or a footprint.

Legal Responsible Agent (RA): The official and/or agency having legal responsibility for the emergency response to a SAR incident. In ICS this person is the "Agency Administrator."

Lock-in: Centering all attention to one aspect to the exclusion of other details.

Outsole: The bottom of the shoe that contacts the ground.

Point **Last Seen (PLS)**: The point the lost person was last seen.

Probability Density (Pden): The ratio of a segment's POA to its physical area.

Probability of Area (POA): The probability (in percentages) that the target or subject is located in a defined area.

Probability of Detection (POD): 1) The percentage of objects that would be detected in a search area if they were in the area. 2) **predictive POD**: A POD that is obtained through prior research 3) **reported POD**: A POD

reported to debriefing officer after a field deployment 4) **adjusted POD**: POD recorded by the debriefing officer taking into consideration the reported POD and other environmental and experience factors. 5) **theoretical cumulative POD**: Cumulative POD obtained through the use of independent probability equation 6) **actual POD**: POD obtained through experimental research with a correction factor for experimentally induced morale enhancement.

Resources: All personnel, services, and major items of equipment available, or potentially available, for assignment to incident tasks on which a status is maintained.

Resource mixing: Application of different resource types to a search sector usually at different times to balance their strengths and weaknesses and raise the actual POD_{cum}.

SAR **incident**: Any situation requiring notification and alerting of the SAR system and which may require SAR mission(s).

Scent article: Any item that the subject has come in contact with, or a secured known location where the subject was last seen.

Scent-discriminating: The ability to differentiate between different scents. In this book it refers to dogs that are trained to be able to tell humans apart by their scent.

Search and Rescue system: An arrangement of components activated as needed to efficiently and effectively aid persons or property in actual or potential distress.

Search and Rescue (SAR): The use of available resources to assist persons and property in potential or actual distress.

Search area: Area assigned by competent authority to be searched.

Sector: A search area in which a search resource may be deployed to accomplish a single sortie or task in a 4-8 hour timespan.

Segment: Often synonymous with search sector. A planning segment consists of several search sectors.

Sign: A disturbance to the environment, whose maker is unknown.

Signcutter: A person who looks for sign, clue, tracks, or disturbances.

Sweep width (W): A measure of "detectability" from search theory not a physical width in the ordinary sense.

Track trap: An area where tracks can be easily detected.

Tracker: An individual who can detect and follow signs of human passage. Sometimes also referred to as a "mantracker" or "sign-cutter".

Tracking dog: A search dog that will follow the ground scent of a person who has passed through an area in which the dog is searching.

Trailing dog: A search dog that will follow the scent trail of a specific individual, after the dog has been allowed to smell an article or object that has been in contact with that individual. The trailing dog is scent-discriminating.

Urban Search: SAR conducted in populated areas.

Index

Other Selected dbS Productions Products

Lost Person Behavior: A Search and Rescue Guide on Where to Look – for Land, Air and Water by Robert J. Koester
ISBN 978-1-879471-39-9 (2008) 416p. (5.5 x 8.5), semi-concealed wiro **$25.00**

Foundations for Awareness, Signcutting and Tracking by Robert Speiden
ISBN 978-0-9817686-0-1 (2009) 268p. (8.5 x 11), paperback   **$35.00**

Urban Search: Managing Missing Person Searches in the Urban Environment by Christopher S. Young and John Wehbring.
ISBN 978-1-879471-38-2 (2007) 352p. (5.5 x 8.5), paperback   **$25.00**

Field Operations Guide for Search & Rescue: Standard Operating Guidelines for Search & Rescue Using the Incident Command System. By Robert J. Koester
ISBN: 1-879471-15-9 (1996) 68p. (8 x 5.5)   **$10.00**

Incident Commander for Ground Search and Rescue: A training course for Incident Commanders by Robert J. Koester
ISBN: 1-879471-22-1 (1997) Student Manual 230p. (8.5 x 11)   **$35.00**
ISBN: 1-879471-21-3 (1999) Instructor Manual 290p. (8.5 x 11)   **$75.00**

Lost Alzheimer's Disease Search Management: A Law Enforcement Guide to Managing the Initial Response and Investigation of the Missing Alzheimer's Disease Subject by Robert J. Koester
ISBN: 1-879471-34-5 (1999) 96p. Three-Ring Binder   **$75.00**

Fatigue : Sleep Management During Disasters and Sustained Operations:
ISBN: 1-879471-17-5 1997 Instructor Manual with overhead masters and MS-Powerpoint Showtime 3.5 disk, 8.5 x11   **$110.00**
ISBN: 1-879471-18-3 1997 Student Manual 58 pages 5.5 x 8   **$10.00**

Order Information

To contact us:

phone/fax   +1.434.293.5502
email   info@dbs-sar.com
online   www.dbs-sar.com
mail   PO Box 1894, Charlottesville, VA 22903